Roy,

I hope you enjoy reading about my life story and find inspiration to share w/ others the importance of practicing healthy financial habits, and recognize the role of financial health in our overall well-being.

From my wellness to yours,

Aileen

NURSING OUR *Financial Health*

Financial Habits for Overall Well-Being

Aileen Ramos

gatekeeper press™

Columbus, Ohio

The views and opinions expressed in this book are solely those of the author and do not reflect the views or opinions of Gatekeeper Press. Gatekeeper Press is not to be held responsible for and expressly disclaims responsibility of the content herein.

Nursing Our Financial Health: Financial Habits for Overall Well-Being

Published by Gatekeeper Press
2167 Stringtown Rd, Suite 109
Columbus, OH 43123-2989
www.GatekeeperPress.com

Copyright © 2022 by Aileen Ramos
All rights reserved. Neither this book, nor any parts within it may be sold or reproduced in any form or by any electronic or mechanical means, including information storage and retrieval systems, without permission in writing from the author. The only exception is by a reviewer, who may quote short excerpts in a review.

Library of Congress Control Number: 2022940141

ISBN (hardcover): 9781662929335
eISBN: 9781662929342

Table of Contents

Acknowledgments iv
Preface v
Disclaimer ix
Introduction x

Chapter 1 Schedule Routine Financial
           Health Assessments 1
Chapter 2 Create SMART for MI Goals to Provide
           Financial Direction 13
Chapter 3 Budget Toward Financial Fidelity 27
Chapter 4 Buyer Be[a]ware of Financial Waste 44
Chapter 5 Living Efficiently Through
           Financial Savviness 55
Chapter 6 Save Yourself to Enhance Your Financial
           Resiliency and Security 66
Chapter 7 Learn to Earn, a Lifelong Investment
           Strategy 81
Chapter 8 Find Financial Reliability Through a
           Career, Not a Job 90
Chapter 9 Financial Generosity, a Sign of Financial
           Wellness and Contentment 100

Conclusion: My Financial Health Summary 111
References 114

Acknowledgments

Through their inspiration, I dedicate this book to:

My late mother, Alice, who taught me the importance of bookkeeping to gain awareness of where my money is going and saving money as a safeguard for any unexpected financial shortcomings.

My father, Armando, for the endless lectures about the worth of having ambitions and goals in life. We are responsible for the choices we make and creating our own destiny.

My husband, Patrick, for the unwavering support and helping me turn my dreams into realities. Thank you for your selfless love.

My son, Jasper, who gives me the courage to pursue endless possibilities.

Preface

2020 was definitely a year of challenges but it was also a year of realization and opportunities for me. I was feeling lost in my career, not sure if it had anything to do with the pandemic since I had to shift my focus to my then five-year-old son as schools closed. I am a type A, goal-oriented, and obsessive list-making person. Before the pandemic, I had my career goals planned out for the next five years, which were:

- Get a job in quality improvement. *Done.* I welcomed in 2020 by working as a quality improvement (QI) specialist.
- Earn a master's degree in business administration or public health. *Done.* I successfully obtained a Master of Business Administration in Healthcare Management (MBA-HM) in April 2020.
- Obtain Certified Professional in Healthcare Quality (CPHQ) certification by December 2020. Not done.
- Earn a Six Sigma Black Belt. Not done.
- Become a Director of Patient Safety and Quality within 3–5 years after earning my MBA-HM. Not done.

As the pandemic took hold, I found my five-year career plan shattered. Suddenly, uncertainties enveloped me. I had no idea what I wanted to do anymore. I was in la-la land when it came to my career. The pandemic was life-altering in many ways on a global level. Society felt halted due to the shutdown of many businesses. Unintentionally, it provided me an opportunity to have ample time to reflect on my life.

We now live in an era in which certain individuals and organizations have no qualms in bombarding us with toxicity, hyper-distractions, and misinformation. The pandemic amplified concerns for mental health issues due to the lack of social interaction. Though social media is a great way to stay connected with families and friends, there is increasing recognition of social media's role in contributing to depression and loneliness (Hunt, Marx, Lipson, and Young, 2018).

I experienced the negativity of social media's impact firsthand. As I read comments posted about the achievements, celebrations, and events I shared, there was always a comment or two that turned my happiness and excitement into guilt, pain, and insecurity. I was not the only one sharing such things on the internet. And yet, the commenters questioned why I was the one gloating. I tried to brush such comments aside, but the hurt lingers as that was never my intent.

It was finally during the pandemic that I made the deliberate decision to detox from social media and declutter my mind; instead of scrolling through Instagram posts and stories and constantly posting what I was doing and eating, I explored life-enriching activities like exercising and reading books. Getting off social media helped me nurture the right—and creative—side of my brain. I read many self-help books, especially those about financial health and personal development.

Preface

This experience was especially fruitful as it occurred at a time where I felt lost in my career. It gave me deeper insight into the inter-connectedness of the various aspects of well-being, especially the role of financial health. As I became more passionate about financial health, I re-joined social media with the caveat of seeking others who shared a similar interest in financial health. In this online community, I found support and encouragement. This feeling rekindled my spirits and emboldened me to find a way to contribute to improving the lives of others. From that inspiration, this book was born.

Growing up, my parents did not shy away from talking about money, especially my mom. I do not come from a wealthy family, but I grew up with abundance of love, care, and advice from my parents: importance of goal setting, budgeting, saving, and sharing, which have been invaluable to #adulting. I applied the teachings I learned growing up into my adulthood that helped me learn to manage my money well.

After graduating from nursing school, my financial health was ailing due to a large amount of student loans. Instead of acclimating habits that would increase my debt, such as justifying retail therapy to cope with the stress and momentarily forget my debt, I consciously made a choice to nurse my ailing financial health. I had a keen awareness that practicing healthy habits of setting financial goals, living efficiently, sticking to a budget plan, and saving money would result in peace of mind, and consequently a happier life. I have always believed that our financial health impacts the health of our overall well-being, and that a healthy finance fosters a healthy well-being. But somehow, many do not see it this way. And this is why I want to help people nurse their financial health.

As a nurse, I live by the guiding question, "how can I contribute to make a difference in someone's life?" During my bouts of feeling lost and not being able to interact with patients and provide direct patient care, my mind was constantly troubled by the question, *what can I do to help?* I truly believe the pandemic made me feel useless as a nurse because I was not in the field helping during the peak of the pandemic because my son was my priority. I sought ways on how I could help and realized I can still help make a difference in someone's life without providing hands-on patient care.

With my MBA-HM, nursing degree, and tried-and-true successful healthy financial habits, I can help people take care of their personal finances, like I help patients manage their pain or swelling after a surgery or trauma. I can help people gain control of their personal finances rather than the other way around. When we make a conscious decision where to spend our money, we establish a sense of freedom. Many people think they need to earn a lot of money in order to be financially healthy. But the truth is, having a lot of money does not automatically make a person healthy financially, especially when they do not know how to manage their personal finances. There are many high earners who have poor financial health due to poor budgeting and/or acclimation to a consumer-driven lifestyle. Becker reviewed the results of a study conducted by PYMNTS and LendingClub and wrote that thirty-six percent of consumers earning more than $250K annually and forty-two percent of consumers earning more than $100K annually lived paycheck to paycheck (2022). No matter where you are in your financial life, I hope this book will be a tremendous help for you.

Disclaimer

This book is not about how to become financially rich. The purpose of this book is to provide insight on how I nursed my and my husband's personal finances to improve and sustain our financial health.

I recognize and understand that each of us are in different situations, and that what worked for me may not work for you. However, I believe being financially healthy is important for everyone. My goal is to help others recognize the value of developing and practicing healthy financial habits. Achieving financial security and freedom will enable us to live life to fulfill our needs, plan for our wants, and prepare us for the unexpected and our uncertainties. By reducing our financial stresses, we can hopefully live a happier life and improve our overall health and well-being.

Through this book, I share my life lessons and practices with the hope that some may find my systems and processes valuable and then apply it to their own personal finances. We all have experiences and lessons. When we share these with the world, it is only then that we can help make a positive change. In his book, *The Seven Decisions*, Andy Andrews writes, "there are generations yet unborn whose very lives depend upon the choices you make because everything you do matters" (2008).

Introduction

"Are you well?" is a simple question. Yet a closer examination of the question reveals that your answer may be deceptively inadequate. This is because the question itself lacks specificity and context as to whether the inquisitor is truly interested in your response. While there is greater focus on our mental and social health when it comes to our overall well-being, our response to this question is most likely based on our physical state of health. Even if you were to factor in all three components of health into your response, your answer would still be inadequate because you forgot one vital component: your financial health. This is a crucial, yet overlooked, aspect to well-being because financial health can negatively or positively impact the other components.

The human body is a miraculous organization composed of atomically intricate and complex systems whose sole purpose is to maintain and achieve homeostasis. For example, when drinking water, our body will only absorb as much water as it needs to maintain proper hydration. If we drank more water than needed, then our body would urinate the excess water. If we drank an inadequate amount of water, our body would send signals to initiate the thirst response for more water. These operations are harmonious, but they are fragile and not infallible.

Extrinsic influences, immunological activity, congenital anomalies, genetic disorders, and/or diseases can interfere or

Introduction

impact our normal bodily functions. Hypercholesteremia is a disease in which we have a high level of cholesterol in the blood stream. High cholesterol is bad because cholesterol buildup can occur along the blood vessels and thereby restrict blood flow. If this buildup occurs in the coronary arteries, it increases the chance that we may suffer a myocardial infarction, i.e., heart attack.

Understanding this disease process and its impact on the normal functioning of the human body is the basis of pathophysiology. Pathophysiology identifies the disease's causes (etiology) and risk factors, its progression within the human body (pathogenesis), the body's experience of the disease (clinical manifestation), and interventions to treat or prevent the disease. A primary etiology of hypercholesteremia is a high-fat diet. For those at risk or newly diagnosed, eating a healthier diet low on fat is a behavioral modification used as the primary intervention to prevent the disease or its progression. If this intervention is unsuccessful or inadequate in treating the disease, medications are available to promote the metabolization of cholesterol.

Medically, our understanding and management of our health centers around the pathogenesis of a disease or illness. It is a prescriptive viewpoint: I have a disease, this is the (likely) cause, and this is how I am supposed to treat it. "Opposite" of pathogenesis is salutogenesis. Salutogenesis focuses on activities and choices that promote well-being. Under this context, we should exercise and eat healthily not because we are trying to prevent (pathogenesis view) diabetes, obesity, or heart disease, but because it will make our bodies more resistant overall (salutogenesis view).

Aaron Antonovsky first developed the idea of salutogenesis, and one key component of this, a "Sense of Coherence" (SOC), focuses on our perception of life and our ability to withstand the various stressors in our life (Mittelmark et al., 2017). Our ability to withstand depends on our ability to comprehend, manage, and find meaningfulness in those stressors. This is especially true when it comes to our financial well-being.

Being financially unwell can contribute to psychologic and physical ailments. Any of these components (financial, psychologic, and physical) can become a catalyst to a feedback loop of cascading negativity if left untreated. For example, mounting debt increases stress, which increases one's blood pressure resulting in a stroke, which causes a loss of income due to reduced physical abilities from the stroke contributing to a state of depression, reducing one's motivation toward physical recovery, etc. Behavioral modifications are necessary to prevent or break this loop.

Consider the following statistics from the FINRA Foundation's 2018 National Financial Capability (NFC) Study (Hasler, 2021)—a survey involving 27,091 American adults that queried the respondents' financial literacy, practices, anxiety, and stress—which illustrated "Americans' ill-preparedness to face financial shocks." Of all the respondents surveyed:

- 53% felt some level of financial anxiety (with 22% of the respondents strongly agreeing that personal finances made them feel anxious)
- 31% were unable to or most likely unable to come up with $2,000 to cover an emergency expense within the next month
- 47% did not have an emergency fund to cover three months of expenses

Introduction

- 36% reported spending entire earnings
- ~ 20% accumulated debt

Unsurprisingly, the COVID-19 pandemic that began in March 2020 (and as of this writing, continues today) compounded the financial difficulties many experienced daily. During the pandemic, many people struggled financially due to job loss, furlough, or resigning from a job to care for a child (or children) due to school closures. A poll of 3,454 U.S. adults illustrated the impact of the coronavirus pandemic (NPR, 2020). Forty-six percent of the respondents reported facing serious financial problems (e.g., depleting savings and paying expenses), and another 46% reported facing some form of job or income loss (of which 68% of those also reported facing serious financial problems).

These statistics highlight the utility of examining the pathophysiology of financial disease and illness. Financial stress is common in almost every household. The 2018 NFC study found that 44% of the respondents stated financial discussions made them feel stressed (Hasler, 2021). Despite being a very common experience and sentiment for many individuals, society has deemed it taboo to openly discuss financial difficulties.

How can we get help when we refuse to talk about our money issues? When we see our doctor, we disclose our physical and mental health problems so we can get the help we need to treat and/or prevent any potential disease. We should treat our financial health the same way. We should not let our fear of shame and/or judgment paralyze us to act and seek the help we need. In my opinion, refusing to discuss financial matters can keep us secluded and uneducated about healthy financial habits and practices that could help us manage our finances better.

Talking about money is vital, especially about ideas on how to better take care of our personal finances.

Just as some individuals are predisposed to certain medical conditions due to inherent factors (race, gender, age, genetics, and/or socioeconomic), these same factors also impact financial health (with genetics referring to generational wealth and connections). Individuals impacted by these factors are undoubtedly less financially healthy than their counterparts. Fortunately, being financially unwell is not a terminal condition.

Though becoming financially unwell can occur suddenly or gradually, becoming financially healthy is a gradual process requiring long-term commitment. This is true even if one was to become suddenly flush with cash (e.g., winning a lotto or receiving an inheritance). It is easier to become financially unwell than financially healthy.

In this book, I will take a somewhat salutogenic approach as I share my perspectives of financial well-being and how my healthy financial habits nursed my financial health. Many people lack the knowledge of how to take care of their personal finances, like something as simple as budgeting. I want to help address financial health as part of our overall well-being. In each chapter, I will be sharing my life lessons and experiences that inspired my financial habits. I will then provide a breakdown of what it is (comprehension), why it is important (meaningfulness), and how I implement it (manageability). These financial habits helped me achieve financial stability and gave me the freedom to live the life I desire without worrying about unexpected expenses. Most importantly, my healthy financial habits helped me attain a healthy well-being (physically, mentally, socially, and financially) and a happier life.

CHAPTER 1

Schedule Routine Financial Health Assessments

Healthy Financial Habit

Financial health assessments provide insight into your current financial health status and help identify opportunities to improve your financial well-being. Performing financial health assessments routinely promotes financial well-being because it serves as a progress report as to your ability to attain and maintain financial health.

Life Inspiration

Many of us go through life with a sense of naivety toward our health. Our physical and mental health are often an afterthought and typically do not become a focal point until the clinical manifestation or inadvertent discovery of a disease. My mother's experience with colon cancer is a prime example of this situation/mentality. One late summer day, she started complaining of severe abdominal pain. I took her to an emergency department, and her providers discharged her for what they thought was a urinary tract infection. The next morning, I came home from work (at the time, I was working night shift) and found her in bed in fetal position because of excruciating pain. I told my dad to take her to a different hospital. My dad later called with news that altered my life forever—my mom had cancer. A biopsy confirmed that she had stage 4 colon cancer as it had already metastasized to her liver.

At the time of her diagnosis, my mom had never gotten screened for colorectal cancer. She was in the age group in which her first screening should have taken place several years prior. Unfortunately, it was not until the year prior to her cancer diagnosis when my mom took greater interest in her health, and by that time, it was too late. My mom tried to live and eat healthily, but she was also averse to going to the doctors. Perhaps it was something she never was accustomed to, growing up in the Philippines. Whatever the reason, I will never know, but her experience with cancer taught me the importance of taking the necessary steps to take care of my health.

Overtime, my understanding of health has evolved. I cannot emphasize this point enough: we must always remember that our health is not only about our physical and psychological states, but that it also encompasses social and financial states as all four components are inter-related. I believe there is a strong correlation between our overall well-being and financial health. For example, obesity has been the focal point for health policy makers as a major risk factor for many chronic diseases. A lot of the interventions on preventing obesity focus on dietary intake and improving sedentary lifestyle. However, obesity could also be a result of poor coping mechanisms (e.g., overeating) when dealing with stress, especially those financial in nature.

Schedule Routine Financial Health Assessments

Comprehensibility

Financial stress can refer to one of two concepts. The first is the psychological anguish one experiences because of one's financial situation. The second reference pertains to competing or mounting expenses that exert tension on one's financial situation. This reference is analogous to the mechanical stress in physics, e.g., stress fractures refer to breaks or cracks in our bones that results from constant force (e.g., runners can develop stress fractures in their legs or feet due to their feet constantly pounding on the pavement). To better distinguish the two, I will use financial anxiety to refer to the psychological anguish and financial tension to the mechanical reference. When a situation involves both financial anxiety and financial tension, I will use financial stress as the descriptor.

This differentiation is necessary because financial anxiety and financial tension can exist independent of each other. For example, despite being in good financial health, one's constant worry about their financial situation is a form of financial anxiety. Such an individual has a low tolerance to stressors. An individual with high tolerance to stressors may not feel financial anxiety despite living paycheck to paycheck (financial tension). Though financial anxiety and financial tension can exist alone, it is often more likely that financial tension triggers financial anxiety (i.e., living paycheck to paycheck is a stressor). The ability to cope with financial stress is dependent on our resiliency and access to appropriate and proper psychological, physical, social, and financial resources.

The ability to cope begins with acknowledging and understanding the very presence and impact of financial stress on our everyday lives. This is because a Capital One® CreditWise®

survey found that "73% of Americans rank their finances as the number one stress in life—more than work (49%) and family (46%)" (Capital One, 2019). From here, we can examine sources of financial stress, especially those pertaining to financial anxiety. The lack of financial literacy is a contributing factor to financial anxiety (Hasler et al., 2021). Fernando (2021) defined financial literacy as "the ability to understand and effectively use various financial skills, including personal financial management, budgeting, and investing." The 2019 Consumer Financial Literacy Survey illustrates a disconnect in understanding one's financial situation. Consider the following statistics from the survey of 2,086 adults (NFCC, 2019):

- 55% of the respondents graded themselves an A or B (on the A to F grading scale) when asked about their knowledge about personal finance, and yet, 58% of the respondents do not have a budget to manage their money.
- 63% of the respondents save less than 11% of their income every year for retirement, but 52% are confident that they have saved enough for retirement.

This disconnect contributes to both forms of our financial stress. For example, as we get closer to retirement, we may start to realize that our retirement savings is not enough to cover our monthly expenses (financial tension), causing anguish and anxiety about the ability to live comfortably in retirement (financial anxiety). This scenario illustrates how financial anxiety is the clinical manifestation of financial tension.

As counterintuitive as it may sound, financial stress provides an opportunity toward our financial well-being. Allowing financial stress to persist has a negative impact psychologically, physically, socially, and financially. This negative impact provides the basis as to why it is meaningful to manage and respond to financial stress.

Meaningfulness

Financial issues have been one of the top offenders affecting people's overall health—including lack of sleep, weakened immune systems, hypertension, and depression (Everyday Health, 2018; Bankrate, 2019 & 2020, as cited in Arnold, 2020; Purdue University, 2020). Is it not mind-boggling that 78% of U.S. adults are not sleeping well because of money problems, yet because money problems are not directly medical in origin, our healthcare system fails to assess financial health during our annual medical exam.

Stress is associated with many serious health problems such as anxiety, depression, heart disease, weight gain or obesity, gastrointestinal problems, diabetes, and other illnesses. Hence, it is equally important to assess our financial health to gain awareness and understand where we stand, and determine any necessary lifestyle changes, such as reducing the frequency of dining out, shopping, etc. Having awareness and understanding of our financial health can help us mitigate potential money-related issues, and consequently reduce stress that could affect our overall wellness.

Manageability

Many of us see our doctor annually for a routine physical health assessment. This gives our doctor the opportunity to screen for a potential disease early on, and prevent such disease from developing, like an increased blood sugar can lead to diabetes without early detection. During our annual exam, depending on the findings, our doctor would educate us about a healthy lifestyle. For example, if our blood sugar is trending up, our doctor would counsel us about the importance of exercise and healthy diet as a prevention.

As a nurse, I have a vital role in promoting lifestyle changes to empower patients to adopt healthy habits. Health promotion is the key principle in preventing many chronic diseases. For example, lack of physical activity poses many health risks, such as weight gain, heart disease, depression, type 2 diabetes, and many other diseases. Our habits do not only affect our physical and mental health, but they also affect our financial health and vice versa. Our health has been hyper-focused on physical and mental needs, and our health care system caters to this. Despite a litany of evidence supporting the negative health consequences of financial distress, there is no medicine or drug to cure this. There is no financial assessment tool incorporated on the health questionnaire we get each year we visit our doctor for a routine wellness exam, as simple as "Is money a problem in your life right now?" And I am not aware of any referrals a doctor can provide should one be experiencing a financial hardship, like a referral to a support group, financial counselor, or simple tools about budgeting.

Financial health assessment is essential to providing greater awareness of one's financial health. This provides an overview of where the financial tension exists, and by creating an appropriate response to that financial tension, one can mitigate financial anxiety. There are many ways to assess our financial health, but three tools that I have incorporated into my routine financial health assessment are based on net worth, debt-to-income

Schedule Routine Financial Health Assessments

ratio, and Power Percentage™. I use these three tools because it provides greater context of my financial situation (Figure 1).

Personal Financial Health Assessment					Date: 01/02/2020
NET WORTH		**DEBT-TO-INCOME (DTI)**		**POWER PERCENTAGE™**	
ASSETS		**PRE-TAX INCOME (Monthly)**		**PRE-TAX INCOME (Monthly)**	
Liquid		Paycheck #1	$ 5,000.00	Paycheck #1	$ 5,000.00
Checking account #1	$ 10,000.00	Paycheck #2	$ 7,250.00	Paycheck #2	$ 7,250.00
Savings account #1	$ 5,000.00	**TOTAL INCOME**	**$ 12,250.00**	**TOTAL INCOME**	**$ 12,250.00**
Checking account #2	$ 500.00				
Savings account #2	$ 30,000.00				
Certificate of Deposit	$ 25,000.00				
Taxable investment	$ 100,000.00				
Illiquid					
529 Plan	$ 65,000.00				
403b	$ 450,000.00				
DRS	$ 120,000.00	**DEBT PAYMENT (Monthly)**		**HEALTHY FINANCIAL ACTIVITIES**	
Roth IRA	$ 30,000.00	Home Mortgage	$ 2,000.00	Retirement Plan Deposit	$ 1,500.00
Property	$ 500,000.00	Car Loan	$ 200.00	Employer Match	$ 250.00
Vehicle #1	$ 10,000.00	Student Loans	$ 500.00	College Fund Deposits	$ 250.00
Vehicle #2	$ 20,000.00	Revolving Debt (Credit Card)	$ -	Savings Deposits	$ 1,500.00
Jewelry	$ 30,000.00	Other Debt	$ -	Other Investment Deposits	$ 500.00
Collectibles	$ 25,000.00	**TOTAL DEBT PAYMENT**	**$ 2,700.00**	Mortgage	$ 2,000.00
TOTAL ASSETS	**$ 1,365,500.00**			Other Monthly Debt Payments	$ 700.00
LIABILITIES				**TOTAL HFA**	**$ 8,700.00**
Home Mortgage	$ 200,000.00				
Car loan	$ 5,000.00				
Student loan	$ 20,000.00				
TOTAL LIABILITIES	**$ 225,000.00**				
NET WORTH	**$ 1,140,500.00**	**DTI (Target < 36%)**	**22.04%**	**Power Percentage™ (Target > 33%)**	**71.02%**

Figure 1. Template of personal financial health assessment with fictional figures.

Net Worth

Our net worth is a good indicator of our overall financial health. Our net worth is the value of our total assets minus our total liabilities. A simple way to understand and calculate our net worth is to subtract how much we *owe* (liabilities) from how much we *own* (assets). For example, if we own a home with a value of $550,000 and we owe $400,000, our net worth is $150,000. To calculate your net worth:

1. Calculate the sum value of all your assets. It helps to make a list of all your assets. Remember, assets can be:
   a. Liquid, which are assets that have stable value, quick cash conversion thereby making it readily available for use. Examples of liquid assets include

cash, savings, certificate of deposit (CD), stocks, and if retired, retirement savings.
  b. Illiquid, which are assets that have dynamic value (i.e., its value can range based on its perception by others) and may take some time to convert into cash. If we own a home, this home is a prime example of illiquid assets because it takes time to sell it. Other examples of illiquid assets include real estate, car, jewelry, and collectible items.
2. Calculate the sum value of all your liabilities. Again, make a list of all your liabilities. Common liabilities include loans (such as mortgage, car, student, and/or personal loans) and credit card debt.
3. Subtract all your liabilities from your assets.

Do not use net worth alone as the overall indicator of financial health. Many college graduates begin their career with a negative net worth. I had $60,000 worth of student loans, and I have read of others who have mortgaged their entire future on six-figure loans. A negative net worth is not necessarily a sign of failure, but it is a starting point for progress. I viewed my student loan as a startup cost necessary to invest in my education that I knew would eventually bring long-term returns.

My starting salary as a nurse was 55% higher than the median wage in the United States. According to the Bureau of Labor Statistics (BLS) of the U.S. Department of Labor (2009), "in 2008, the U.S. median wage was $15.57 per hour or $32,390 per year." Being a nurse provided me the financial advantage to pay off my debt and build wealth in a quicker manner than other college graduates in different industries.

Schedule Routine Financial Health Assessments

It took me many years to develop my financial literacy to where it is now. At the time I first started working, my primary focus was paying off my student loans and not increasing my net worth (though, technically, paying off debt does increase net worth incrementally). Net worth gives us a snapshot of our financial health, which allows us to detect financial ailments or liabilities, and gives us the opportunity to rehabilitate, modify, or improve our financial habits and lifestyle to prevent further financial harm. Knowing I owed $60,000, I willfully made the decision not to overspend and prioritized paying off my student loans while simultaneously saving for unexpected life event(s). As we pay off our loans, our net worth should naturally increase (so long as we make the conscious decision to practice healthy financial habits that avoid overspending and debt accumulation, but instead focus on saving and investing money to increase our net worth and consequently build wealth).

Debt-to-Income Ratio

Debt-to-income ratio (DTI) is another way I track the progress of our financial health. The lower the DTI, the healthier our finances are. Our DTI compares the amount of our debt to our income. Lenders often utilize DTI to determine how comfortable they are with providing financial assistance to a consumer. DTI provides a snapshot of our financial health, and it helps lenders determine our ability to repay a loan on a scheduled basis. The *lower* the DTI, the higher the chance is that a financial institution will approve us for our desired loan amount. In contrast, a *higher* DTI is an indication that we need much of our current income to cover our existing debt. To the lender, this decreases our ability to repay any new loans and means we are more at risk of defaulting on a loan than someone with a lower DTI. Many lenders prefer a DTI ratio less than or equal to 36% because it suggests we have enough income to repay the loan monthly.

Another way to view this is that if your monthly income is $10K with a DTI of 40%, then you are spending $4,000 ($10K x 40% = $4,000) a month repaying off debt and have $6,000 of your monthly income that could be used for new debt. However, if you were to take on new debt (such as buying a new car), this lessens the amount of income you have for other necessities. This scenario illustrates the risk of lenders providing funding to consumers with higher DTI.

To calculate your DTI, perform the following steps:

1. Calculate the sum of your monthly recurring debt payments. This includes all your credit card payments (based on the minimum payment due) and scheduled loan (for mortgage, car, student, and/or personal loans) repayment plans.
2. Determine your gross monthly income, i.e., your monthly income before all the withholdings (e.g., federal and/or state taxes, social security, retirement, etc.).
3. Divide your total monthly recurring debt payments (step 1) by your gross income (step 2).
4. [Optional] Multiply the result by 100%. This is an aesthetic step that displays the result as a percentage, which makes it easier to read and comprehend.

Schedule Routine Financial Health Assessments

Power Percentage™

A few years ago, I came across an interesting article in *USA Today*'s Money section about Peter Dunn's Power Percentage™ formula. This is the first formal financial tool that I had ever used, and I have adopted it as part of my routine financial health assessment. This tool provides an overview of how we allocate our income toward healthy financial activities monthly. Examples of healthy financial activities, according to Dunn (2022), include savings used for retirement, college funds, and investments and monthly debt payments. A healthy financial lifestyle has a score between 21%–35%, and a score greater than 35% reflects someone who has a mastered financial lifestyle. As of the end of 2021, my husband and I (since we share our finances together) have a Power Percentage™ score of 57%. I highly suggest you visit https://petetheplanner.com to learn more about this tool so you can begin to apply it to your annual financial health assessment.

Summary

Financial stress is unavoidable, but its impact on our financial health is all dependent on our ability to resist and respond. Developing this ability begins with understanding your current financial situation. A routinely performed financial health assessment can provide an overview of your financial situation at any given time. There are three tools that I incorporated into my financial health assessment. When our DTI was high, my husband and I implemented necessary lifestyle changes to lower it. As our DTI improved, we saw our net worth and Power

Percentage™ score improve because we had more income to allocate to healthier financial activities. Focusing on healthier financial activities strengthened our ability to respond and withstand financial stress, which has been fundamental to our ability to create overall wealth and health.

CHAPTER 2

Create SMART for MI Goals to Provide Financial Direction

Healthy Financial Habit

Creating SMART for MI goals utilizes structure, direction, and an emotional desire to promote accountability toward attaining and maintaining financial well-being.

Life Inspiration

Deeply rooted in me since my childhood was the importance of having an ambition. When I was growing up in the Philippines, my dad would take me and my siblings on 5 a.m. weekend walks along the business strip of Magsaysay Street in Olongapo City. These walks were not meant for exercise, but rather to showcase life's difficulties. Walking alongside the throngs of people sleeping on the streets, my dad warned that being homeless could be our reality if we did not listen, work hard, and do well in school. Through these walks, he ingrained within me a strive for a better life.

Nursing Our Financial Health

In the Philippines, my dad grew up in poverty, which was an experience he did not wish for me and my siblings. There were days as a child in which he scavenged for empty cans and bottles to sell just to have money for school lunch. He later shined shoes on the streets for anyone passing by. The difficult environment that raised my dad did not deter him from achieving his desire for a better future. He worked his way out of poverty as he entered adulthood with diligence and perseverance. He first found a job as a security officer. This opened the door to becoming a police officer (along with being a karate instructor as a side hustle). He utilized this experience and self-studied his way to become a supervisor of criminal scene investigators at the former U.S. Naval Base Subic Bay. Unfortunately, two significant events derailed his career trajectory: Mt. Pinatubo's eruption in June 1991 and the naval base's closure in November 1992.

After the base's closure, my dad took a position as a director of security in Manila. Manila is 96 miles and about a two-and-a-half-hour drive from where we lived. For this reason, my dad stayed in Manila for the week and came home to us on the weekend. My dad hated this situation. Deciding to be closer to home, my dad tried farming watermelons to supplement the income from my mom's general store. His pride beamed brighter each day watching his carefully-grown watermelons. As harvesting day soon approached, a typhoon wreaked havoc on the watermelons not long before harvesting day and completely devasted my dad and his pride. These moments convinced my dad that we needed a new start. Fortunately, my dad's previous work with the U.S. Navy was crucial in getting our family's U.S. special immigrant visa approved.

Create SMART for MI Goals to Provide Financial Direction

We flew into Seattle, Washington, in 1996 to begin our new life. My dad's goal was to resume his career with the U.S. Navy, though he was fully aware this would not be immediate. The U.S. federal government required its prospective employees be U.S. citizens and physically reside in the United States for at least five years. Despite knowing this requirement, my parents believed the opportunity to live in the United States was worth the sacrifice and the patience. My dad accepted our economic hardships as reality, but he did not consider it an impediment to future success. His employment opportunities were steppingstones toward the career he desired.

He first worked as a production line worker at an outdoor equipment and apparel company making minimum wage. Eventually, he secured a position as a security officer at a major hospital in downtown Seattle. This was more aligned with his previous career in the Philippines, but he still was not content. My dad desired to resume his service with the U.S. federal government because he knew this would help him tremendously with his retirement life. With persistence, he got the opportunity he desired as a civilian law enforcement officer at the U.S. Naval Station Everett. My dad was in line for a promotion to captain. Unfortunately, it was at a time when my mom was diagnosed with terminal cancer, and my dad declined the promotion despite the urging from his superior officer. He instead retired early as a lieutenant officer to care for my dying mom. To this day, my dad never regretted his decision to forsake his professional dreams for my mom. He was very much proud of his career accomplishments and is now enjoying retirement back in the Philippines.

My dad's experience gave me motivation and inspiration to succeed in life. It became customary for me to routinely lay out various types of dreams. These dreams ranged from finishing college to getting my dream purse and car. However, I learned that even with a new job, such dreams were not easily within my reach. Fulfilling those dreams involved money, in some way or form, that I did not yet have. A tuition bill followed my college diploma in the mail. My dream purse cost more than my first paycheck, and my dream car cost the same as my annual salary. It was very easy to become stressed, discouraged, and amiss, especially when we compare our situation to those around us who are more fortunate. So why still have ambitions, and how then do we achieve our ambitions and dreams when we have nothing to begin with? The answer is to convert your ambitions into goals.

Comprehensibility

Ambition and goals are often synonymous, but they in fact have significant differences in meaning and applications. Consider the following statements: "I *want* to be wealthy" versus "I *will be* wealthy." Think of ambition as the desired state as in the former statement. To be famous, to be successful, and to be healthy are other common desires, dreams, and wants that people often express. Goals, on the other hand, represent a planned achievement of one's ambition. The latter statement expressed this.

Although ambition is the basis of all goals, ambitions do not require attainment of those goals. The ambition to be wealthy is a common desire for many. It is the reason state lotteries are so popular, especially when the winnings get closer and closer to a billion dollars. For the lucky winner, it is a quick "rags to riches" story, as the saying goes. For those who are not as lucky, my dad demonstrated how sheer perseverance and hard work could also lead to a similar story, albeit not as quickly.

It is easy to assume that becoming wealthy automatically makes us financially healthy. This is a misconstrued fact. Financial health is not based on our monetary wealth, but on how we nurse, or take care of, our finances to grow our wealth while withstanding and addressing financial distress. If "rags to riches" is possible, then so, too, is "riches to rags." Such a story probably occurs more frequently and/or suddenly due to poor financial habits. Avoiding this possibility requires: 1) changing one's ambition to be financially healthy rather than wealthy, and 2) *creating* goals to attain and maintain financial wellness. I am emphasizing "creating" because this process requires serious thought and investment. When properly constructed, these financial goals offer guidance and purpose on nursing your finances, as well as a more predictable and efficient manner in realizing one's ambition than solely relying on luck and/or perseverance and hard work.

Meaningfulness

Without financial goals, we are at risk for developing or continuing poor financial habits. Someone who has a financial goal to pay off a $10,000 credit card debt will direct extra income toward that debt. Someone with the same debt but without a financial goal will find temptation to spend that extra income instead. Without a financial goal to guide them, this individual's habits will further exacerbate their dire financial situation.

For those with a financial goal, the ability to prevent, address, or escape financial distress is all dependent on the quality of the financial goal's construction. Recall that a goal is composed of an outcome and a plan of action. Your financial goals (and goals in general) need to have a solid structure of both components. Flaws in either composition or action plan place the financial goal at risk to collapse or for us to abandon it. Let's re-examine the following goal statement, "I will be wealthy," and review a couple of component flaws and their impact on financial health.

Attaining wealth is the expected outcome of achieving such a goal. The flaw with this outcome is its immeasurability and lack of specifics. Without a clear definition of "wealthy," an individual will never know when they attain this goal and will find the time, effort, and resources wasted in the long run. A lack of specificity on how to attain the goal also contributes to the wasted time, effort, and resources. A properly constructed financial goal is supposed to provide guidance and direction. Without this, an individual's plan could be illogical (e.g., trying to win the lottery weekly), sporadic (e.g., saving money intermittently), arbitrary (i.e., trying various ways to save money or earn more income), or chaotic (i.e., any combination of the previous three). Time, effort, and resources are valuable commodities. Poorly constructed goals utilize these commodities improperly.

This does not mean that poorly constructed goals are unattainable. If you spent $100 a week on lottery tickets, you have a greater chance of winning the lottery than if you were to only play a couple times a year. And if you were to hit the

Create SMART for MI Goals to Provide Financial Direction

jackpot, you could state that you reached your goal of becoming wealthy. However, if you did not hit the jackpot, you just wasted and lost $5,200 for the year. Now imagine that instead of trying to win big, you focus on winning small. Investing the $100 weekly in an investment that has reliably offered a 10% rate of return provides a more reliable means of becoming wealthy. This strategy makes better use of your valuable commodities and will strengthen your financial health instead of jeopardizing it.

Our psychologic, physical, social, and financial health are all intertwined. Anything that negatively impacts one will negatively impact the others. What is the impact of poorly constructed financial goals on your health? If we return back to the goal of being wealthy by spending $100 a week on lottery tickets, dedicating that much money on the lottery will place us in financial constraint if we do not have the means to afford this approach. We may find ourselves so financially constrained that we become unable to pay off our rent. This lack of money can be a source of stress and depression. This may raise our blood pressure and place us at greater risk of stroke. As this illustrates, it entraps us in a negative spiral of psychologic, physical, social, and financial distress unless addressed as soon as possible if not immediately.

On the other hand, utilizing and committing to properly constructed financial goals promote health in various ways. It will guide us into developing and practicing sound financial habits. As our financial health improves, we may find relief with mental stress often associated with finances. Less stress reduces the risks of physical and medical ailments such as hypertension, heart disease, etc. Positive changes to any of these various aspects of health have a positive influence on the other.

Manageability

As I mentioned earlier, a poorly constructed goal leads or contributes to the inability to escape from financial distress. You may have heard of SMART goals, which is an acronym and mnemonic that literally describes the key elements of a properly constructed, or smart, goal. Figures 2.1 and 2.2 are a couple of infographics that illustrate those elements. There is some inconsistency in what each of the letters represent as various organizations and individuals have their own interpretation.

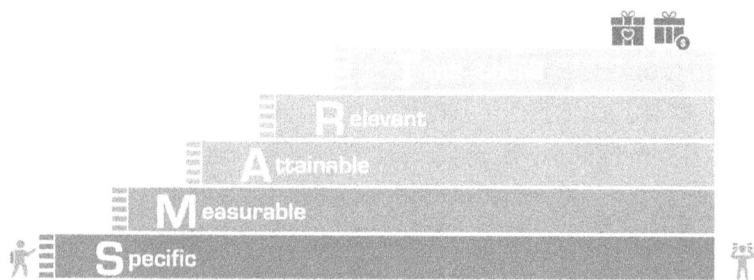

Figure 2.1. Components of a SMART goal.

When applying this concept to your financial health, your financial goals must be specific, measurable, attainable/actionable, relevant/realistic, and timebound (The Coaching Tools Company, 2021; Indeed Editorial Team, 2021). Consider my following SMART financial goal: I will save money on tuition by obtaining my MBA in Healthcare Management through WGU and completing one to two courses per month, which would enable me to complete the online program within one year. Breaking this SMART goal down, we find that this goal is:

Create SMART for MI Goals to Provide Financial Direction

- Specific. Getting an MBA was an ambition of mine, but I wanted to obtain it in the most cost-efficient manner. Completing the MBA program as a full-time student at WGU, which is an online university, in one year provides significant savings on tuition when compared to the average cost and time of other MBA programs.
- Measurable. Obtaining my diploma provides proof that I accomplished my SMART goal. To ensure I kept myself on track, I set a milestone to complete one to two courses per month.
- Attainable/realistic, actionable, and relevant. I combined these two because depending on what you want the A and R to represent, being attainable and realistic are very similar. My SMART goal was attainable and realistic for me because I had taken a sabbatical from my career and had the luxury of time to go to school full time. This gave me the necessary time to focus all my energy on school. Compared to other MBA programs, WGU gave me greater freedom and flexibility to structure the program to best fit my schedule. Lastly, this financial goal was relevant to my nursing career because an MBA in healthcare management reflects professional development and would further advance my career toward healthcare administration and leadership.
- Timebound. Goals require a deadline, and in this case, I gave myself a year to complete WGU's program, which was equivalent to two semesters.

I found that SMART goals provided a nice structure, but I also found that it was too objective. For this reason,

I developed my own modification: SMART *for MI* goals (Figure 2.2). The addition of the prepositional phrase is a play on words as *MI* represents *motivated and inspired*. Motivation and inspiration provide the necessary fuel for us to carry on the work to achieve our goals.

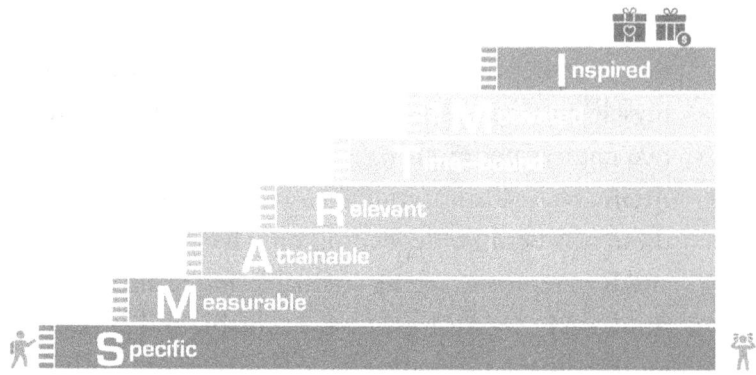

Figure 2.2. Motivating and inspiring factors help achieve SMART goals.

What makes being motivated and inspired critical to goal creation? The Heath Brothers (2010) highlight the importance of ensuring the rider and the elephant are in sync when navigating a path or journey involving change. The rider and the elephant represent two types of individuals: those who think with their brains and those who think with their hearts. Successful change management is dependent on the symbiotic relationship between the two such that the logical rider and the emotive elephant can journey along the same path.

Although *Switch* (Heath & Heath, 2010) is about managing interpersonal relationships in dealing with change, I found that their teachings are very applicable to my own intrapersonal relationship. Each of us has elements of the rider and the

Create SMART for MI Goals to Provide Financial Direction

elephant, and internal conflict arises when our heart "thinks" differently from our brain. Recall those times when we wished we had listened to our gut feeling when answering a test or whenever the results did not turn out like what we expected. When goals are creative but not logical, the creativity may make accomplishing the goal too difficult and increases the likelihood of abandonment. Similarly, goals based on emotions may look and feel good initially, but we may lose interest in them when a sense of defeat or difficulty develops.

SMART provides a logical and rational structure for our goal, and *for MI* provides the emotional investment for us to want to accomplish it. However, we must recognize that accomplishing goals is not an individualistic effort as there is benefit in sharing our goals with the people whom we trust to help us stay accountable. Many times, I wanted to give up writing this book. Thankfully, my husband did not let me. He even saved multiple copies of my book's manuscript in the event that I ever deleted it. This is a prime example of motivation. Unlike inspiration, motivation is external in origin and refers to our support system. These are the people we trust who can help us take the burden during times of difficulty and encourage us to continue and overcome any obstacle.

Inspiration, on the other hand, comes from within us. It is that fire within us that seeks to improve or change. Goals are based on ambition, which means ambition is the inspiration for our goals. With this SMART for MI goal, I was able to complete my whole program in 11.5 months. It provided me a clear path of where to devote my focus, time, and energy. My SMART for MI goal gave me a means to track my progress, and every month, I felt accomplished knowing I attained my established milestones. Each month, my motivation got stronger as I neared the end of completing the program.

To help me better track my financial goals—and my life in general—I started to use the Bullet Journal methodology to document it all (Figure 2.3). This analog system developed by Ryder Carroll (2018) allowed me to organize and take note of "what's important, why it's important, and then figure out how to best pursue those things" in notebooks. Because of my self-discipline, I have the tools and mindset to create various goals on a daily, weekly, monthly, and even yearly basis for me. Before adopting this method, my journaling and note-keeping techniques were chronologically based. If I wanted to remember an idea or a memory, I had to remember the exact date those occurred on or else I would be reading my journals, page by page, until I found it. Instead of using dates as the primary means of organization, the Bullet Journal incorporates an index page to group entries based on topics. This makes it easier to find and review previous entries, even if that information is in a different journal. Because of this organizational advantage, I tracked my life more efficiently and ensured accountability with achieving established goals, especially my financial ones.

A study on goal setting by Dr. Gail Matthews, a psychology professor at Dominican University in California, found that "[we] are 42 percent more likely to achieve [our] goals if [we] write them down" (Matthews, 2007; Gardner & Albee, 2015). One way the Bullet Journal enabled me to organize my goals is through the creation of my five-year plan. Once I constructed several SMART for MI goals, I aligned them into a five-year plan (which is really a SMART for MI goal itself) to provide a better outlook to my future and a bird's eye view of action

Create SMART for MI Goals to Provide Financial Direction

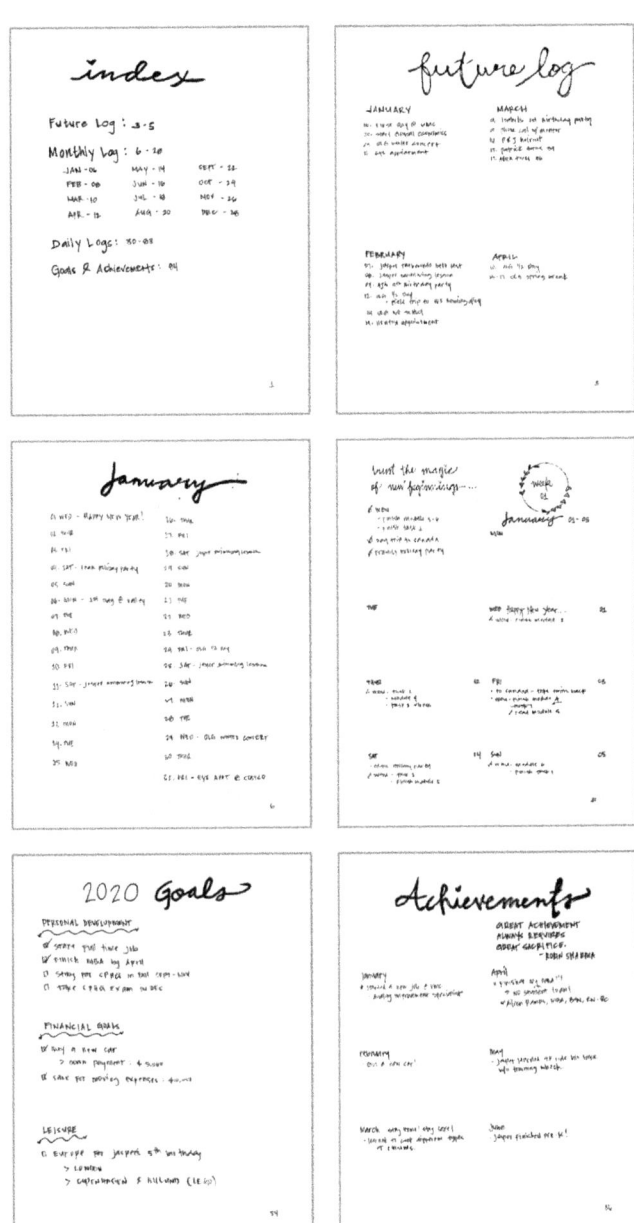

Figure 2.3. Samples of my Bullet Journal collections.

items I need to complete to achieve my future goal(s). Creating this yearly action plan kept me accountable and ensured I did not procrastinate or veer off course of the plan. Seeing my list of action items gave me purpose and direction on how I spent my day, and it motivated me further every time I checked an item off the task list.

Summary

I truly believe establishing financial goals is crucial to living the life we desire. However, this is easier said than done. Maintaining our personal finances requires a great deal of self-discipline, and it is very easy to get off track. If we can commit to our financial goals and plans, we will set ourselves up for long-term benefits in our overall life. When we are committed to achieving our financial goal(s)—for example, saving for retirement, emergency fund, vacation, home, child's college education—we are more bound to being responsible in how we handle our finances. By managing our finances responsibly, we allow ourselves to live with less stress and have more freedom in life. We have more control over our income knowing that it will not disappear like a bubble because we did not let debt take over our life.

CHAPTER 3

Budget Toward Financial Fidelity

Healthy Financial Habit

It is very easy to splurge based on having a high credit card limit or a recent deposit of your paycheck. Even the smallest of purchases, when combined, can chip away at your financial resources and lead you into distress. By creating and utilizing a monthly and annual budget, you become accountable to your daily needs, wants, and financial SMART for MI goals. This healthy financial habit develops and promotes financial fidelity to prevent financial distress.

Life Inspiration

My late mother had a mini store inside our house in the Philippines. I grew up watching her calculate the money coming in and the money going out. She always kept a record of everything in her notebook. Helping at my mom's store was my first formal introduction to math. Counting the coins and bills in the cashier box and providing change to the customers,

I learned addition and subtraction before even attending elementary school.

After moving to the United States, my mom continued her budgeting practice. She had a designated notebook where she kept a record of my dad's income and the monthly expenses. She always talked to me about the importance of knowing where the money goes and keeping record of it. She always had a plan on how to spend the money. She was not an impulsive consumer because she strictly followed her budget plan. Unless she had a way of making it fit into her budget, my mom would only buy what was on her shopping list and nothing more.

When she received her diagnosis of stage 4 colon cancer, I assumed the responsibilities of managing my parents' personal finances. I took over my mom's budget notebook and followed her plan. Even while bedridden in a hospital and weakened from the chemotherapy, my mom knew exactly which bills were due and how much money was available to pay them. I was impressed with how well she programmed her built-in system of budgeting into her brain.

I felt so fortunate to have a mom who accustomed me in creating a financial plan and being mindful on how I spent my money. I adopted her budgeting system and purchased my own notebook to keep record of my income and expenses, which I later migrated into an Excel spreadsheet.

Budgeting provides a bird's eye view of my finances. With the practice of manually entering the amount of my income, and each expense I had to pay each month, it trained my mind to have a mental image of my personal financial statement's income and expenses; I know exactly how much is going in and going out, which helped me become cognizant of my spending.

Budgeting is my safety net against impulsive spending, whether it be for shopping or eating out.

Comprehensibility

Do you recall what you did with your first paycheck? Getting money is a great feeling and celebrating your first paycheck with a splurge probably felt satisfying. Unfortunately, many people fail to realize or learn too late that just because they can make a purchase does not mean they can afford it. Spending is easy. Getting into debt is easier, and making unaffordable purchases is a fast track to debt. Furthermore, affordability is not just about that moment of purchase, but the future impact of that purchase. Will this purchase deplete you of funds to pay other expenses?

It seems counterintuitive to be able to make a purchase when we lack funds in our checking account. And yet, financial institutions have made a profit in allowing consumers to do so. The FinHealth Spend Report 2021 estimated that Americans spent $12.4 billion on overdraft fees (Greene et al., 2021). Overdraft fees are examples of wasted money that are largely preventable with budgeting.

Thankfully, there's a very easy formula that you can use to nurse your finances. By subtracting your total expenses from your total income for a particular period (typically, monthly), you will have an idea of how much or little money you have. Accounting labels this as net income, but I like to think of it as discretionary income—as my budget already accounts for various savings and investments—income for discretionary purposes. The smaller your discretionary income, the more likely you are either living paycheck to paycheck, or that you are in the stages of recuperating or rehabilitating your financial health. It takes a lot of patience and extreme amount of dedication to increase your discretionary income because it takes time to do so. Do not be disheartened, stay the course, and when you become discouraged, look to your SMART for MI goals. What I do not want to see from you is a negative discretionary income. This means your expenses outweigh your income. If you do not address this immediately, your financial distress will result in financial bankruptcy.

Your budget is more than just knowing the discretionary income. It is about knowing how your income is being utilized to finance your life. Knowing your budget can provide insight into the impact of a future purchase, gift, or unexpected expense on your current financial situation; it provides insight into what you need to maintain your current lifestyle as well as guidance on what you will need financially if you wish for a different lifestyle. No matter what, financial well-being begins with an ambition and commitment to generating greater net or discretionary income.

The quickest solution to this is supplementing your income with an additional job, working additional hours, and/or getting an increase in your pay either through a raise or finding another job with better pay. However, your budgets should first be based on your current income. In fact, it is quite advantageous to maintain this budget even as your income increases because your net income will be larger. Simply put, increases with your income does not justify increasing your expenses.

Some expenses, such as rent or mortgage payments, are static, predictable, and required. These expenses are nonnegotiable, meaning you cannot unilaterally lower your payment. When you compile and analyze your expenses, you will need to determine which of those are "needs" and which are "wants." Categorizing your expenses in this manner will help you determine which expenses are not necessities for daily living, and it makes it easier for you to adjust or eliminate what you spend.

When necessary, you must recognize that wants are expenses in which you could live without. However, one difficulty in budgeting is the decision-making process on how to make these adjustments. These adjustments all require some level of sacrifice, but you need to make that of what and how. For example, during your review of your budget expenses, say you find that you spend $5 a day on coffee (about $150 a month). Reducing your coffee consumption to every other day now has increased your net income by at least $75. But reducing your coffee consumption requires commitment and adherence or else that money realized becomes wasted.

These adjustments do not mean that you need to be a penny pincher. On the contrary, I discuss various strategies in subsequent chapters that will help bring your expenses down by focusing on financial efficiency and waste reduction. Like your financial goals, your budgets must be realistic. It is admirable to have a greatly positive net income as soon as possible, but not at the expense of it severely limiting your quality of life. It is appropriate to budget a reward for yourself.

Rewarding yourself is necessary because the most difficult thing about budgeting is maintaining commitment to your budget. It is very easy for us to drift back into our old habits. Using the coffee buying example from above, you may start off only buying every other day, but one bad day may tempt you to buy coffee on a coffee-free day. This cheat day may happen once a week at first, but you soon end up buying it every day again.

Sticking to a budget is not easy and requires a conscientious effort. That's why having a SMART for MI goal will help with this endeavor. The more frequently you do this, the more habitual it becomes. I typically set aside at least an hour every two weeks to review my budget and adjust as needed to ensure I am on track with my financial goals. What has simplified this process for me is the consistency of my budget each month by organizing my income, expenses, and savings chronologically in accordance with its due date. Having a consistent budget helps me understand my finances for the whole year. I can easily point out how much I can save for the whole year and identify how much to set aside for vacations and other splurges, such as birthday and anniversary gifts, without draining my savings account.

Budgeting is a necessary tool as you strive for financial well-being. Budgeting is a life-altering process, and for this reason, it takes time and patience. But as you become more proficient with your budget and understanding your finances, you will soon realize that budgeting not only addresses short-term expenses, but it is also useful in planning and forecasting long-term liabilities. As your liabilities decrease, the more of your net income you can allocate to your financial goals and personal wants. Budgeting is therefore the key to helping you attain your financial goals, and it is why you need to make it a priority.

Meaningfulness

Have you ever or have you known people who are constantly tracking how many calories they consume throughout the day to lose or gain weight? Calorie counting can be useful for weight modification so long as you remain dedicated and committed to it. To me, budgeting is like calorie counting. Our recommended daily calorie intake varies between 1200–2000 depending on our activity level, i.e., sedentary vs. active. If we intake more than 2000 calories daily, we are at risk for weight gain. In a budgeting concept, if we spend more than our budget, for example, $2000, we will incur debt. To prevent weight gain, we become conscious of what we eat and avoid overeating, and budgeting employs a similar notion: we become aware of our spending habits and avoid overspending to prevent debt accumulation.

When money becomes an issue in our lives, like when we are not able to pay for unexpected expenses, we experience financial stress. Stress from any source can increase our risk for diabetes, heart disease, and stroke (Wojcik & Kang, 2022; Lloyd et al., 2005). We use medications to treat medical conditions like diabetes and hypertension. While there are no medications to treat stress, there are tools available to help manage the stress. Budgeting is a vital financial tool to nursing your financial well-being, and I have found it fundamental to achieving my desires in life while living a healthy and less stressful life. With an effective budgeting plan, we can make sure that we have funds for both expected and unexpected expenses. Life becomes less stressful when we are well prepared. Our financial management has a direct correlation with our stress level and health.

One of my professional ambitions was to "stop" working. Not indefinitely, but I wanted to take a sabbatical and reset my mind from the stresses and rigors of work. I would use my sabbatical to rejuvenate my whole being, contemplate my career plans, and explore the world with my family. I created a SMART for MI goal for my sabbatical as I knew that this would be a drastic change, especially on our finances. I was quite anxious in submitting my resignation, though my managers and colleagues were very supportive of my decision.

My sabbatical from working full time to travel and have adventures was a dream come true. It was also one of the best investments I have made in my life. It has been a joy to watch my son grow and witness his eagerness to learn new things. I had the time of my life exploring with him, and though he is constantly asking questions about everything, I have learned to appreciate his curiosity and desire to learn. We have had so much fun discovering new things as we connected with nature, visiting national parks, zoos, and museums. We enjoyed traveling the world and eating (especially desserts) and learning about different cultures. Experiences are invaluable, and I was able to deposit many to my family's memory bank. The only way we were able to experience all of this and fulfill my goal and this dream was because of my budgeting practices.

My family's budget was always based on one income being able to cover the expenses. I started this practice when my husband and I got married. At first, this was a safety net if one of us became debilitated. I placed too much worry about ensuring that the surviving spouse and our son would be financially comfortable. This fear caused me to develop hesitancy in increasing our expenses (such as buying a more expensive house) because I did not want it to place undue burden on the surviving family members. Over time, as my confidence grew with an improved sense of financial well-being, I learned to let go of this fear. My budgeting practices ingrained in me financial empowerment that prepared us financially for my sabbatical and other financial stressors like the pandemic.

Planning for my sabbatical required a lot of resolve and commitment. In preparation for my sabbatical, I altered our budget to maximize our savings by further reducing our expenses by modifying our lifestyle. I discuss more about these modifications in my chapter about financial efficiency. One example of our lifestyle modification included meal planning for the week to reduce the number of times we ate out. My sabbatical is a testament to my family's self-discipline and dedication to our financial well-being.

This budget strategy allowed me to take my sabbatical, but it also allowed us to survive and thrive during the COVID pandemic. The pandemic was and continues to be unfortunate on many levels, so I am fortunate that it did not severely impact us financially. I recognize that we were in a financially advantageous position because our chosen careers as nurses provided job security. However, my budget allowed us to avoid the financial stress that befell many others and navigate and adjust to the pandemic's continuous political-socioeconomic impact. I had just started a new position several months before the COVID-19 pandemic became official but left in the spring to better attend to my son's education as his school had moved to remote learning. This was not a difficult decision for us financially because our budget was not dependent on two incomes. Furthermore, we found opportunities to reduce our expenses further such as freezing our gym membership and working out from home. The travel restrictions placed to help curb the pandemic also gave us an opportunity to reallocate those budgeted expenses to our other savings.

Going into the third year of the pandemic, I have not yet returned to working full time. Our total income is about 25% less than what it was before my sabbatical, but our net worth has doubled since. Our family's budget maximized our income effectively because we adhered to our plan and avoided lifestyle inflation though we could afford it. We have been able to replenish our various savings that we had shortchanged at the beginning of the pandemic, and we started investing. My family's budget allowed us to make the best of a difficult event. We saw a significant increase in our net worth, enhanced our financial well-being, and are more attuned to our overall well-being.

Manageability

Although I enjoy my Bullet Journal, my budget is one that I keep on a spreadsheet due to ease of use. Calculations are automatic, and it is easier to track where I am with my budget. I am constantly reviewing and tracking my expenses to ensure I do not get over budget unless necessary. I am also constantly seeking ways to improve how I organize my budgeting spreadsheet (Figure 3.1).

In addition to my chronological income and expense spreadsheet, I recently started organizing monthly all the

BUDGET 2022				
INCOME		Annual		Monthly
Paycheck A	$	48,000.00	$	4,000.00
Paycheck B	$	72,000.00	$	6,000.00
Less Savings/Investments				
Roth IRA x2	$	12,000.00	$	1,000.00
Monthly savings	$	42,000.00	$	3,500.00
AVAILABLE INCOME	$	66,000.00	$	5,500.00
EXPENSES				
Fixed (Needs)				
Mortgage	$	24,000.00	$	2,000.00
HOA	$	4,800.00	$	400.00
Life insurance	$	720.00	$	60.00
Car insurance	$	1,560.00	$	130.00
Cell phone bill	$	1,800.00	$	150.00
Internet	$	900.00	$	75.00
Subscriptions	$	360.00	$	30.00
Variable (Needs)				
Grocery	$	9,600.00	$	800.00
Gas	$	4,800.00	$	400.00
Utilities	$	4,200.00	$	350.00
Discretionary (Wants)				
Shopping/Dining	$	3,600.00	$	300.00
Self-care (massage, haircut)	$	2,400.00	$	200.00
Gifts	$	1,200.00	$	100.00
TOTAL EXPENSES	$	59,940.00	$	4,995.00
DISCRETIONARY INCOME	$	6,060.00	$	505.00

Figure 3.1. Template of my budget layout with fictional figures.

expenses in categories like grocery, gas, eating out, and shopping. This organization provides me a better understanding where I am spending my money most and which month of the year I am spending the most. I know from the top of my head without even looking at my spreadsheet that March is my most expensive month because it is when we usually pay our taxes (we do not wait until April so we can get it out of the way), when our car registration tabs are due, my and my husband's birthday, and our nursing license renewal.

Knowing in which month I will be spending most helps me prepare for the expenses and make sure I have the funds for it. With this new organization of the expenses, I can do an end-of-year review to plan for the upcoming year (Figure 3.2). It helps me see which category I spent most on and determine whether it is something that I can plan to spend less on for the upcoming year, especially if it's not a necessity.

	January		February		End-of-Year Totals	
INCOME	Budgeted	Actual	Budgeted	Actual	Budgeted	Actual
Paycheck A	$ 4,000.00	$ 4,000.00	$ 4,000.00	$ 4,000.00		
Paycheck B	$ 6,000.00	$ 6,000.00	$ 6,000.00	$ 6,000.00		
Other	$ -	$ 200.00	$ -	$ -		
Less Savings/Investments						
Roth IRA x2	$ 1,000.00	$ 1,000.00	$ 1,000.00	$ 1,000.00		
Monthly savings	$ 3,500.00	$ 3,500.00	$ 3,500.00	$ 3,500.00		
AVAILABLE INCOME	$ 5,500.00	$ 5,700.00	$ 5,500.00	$ 5,500.00	$ 11,000.00	$ 11,200.00
EXPENSES						
Fixed						
Mortgage	$ 2,000.00	$ 2,000.00	$ 2,000.00	$ 2,000.00		
HOA	$ 400.00	$ 400.00	$ 400.00	$ 400.00		
Life insurance	$ 60.00	$ 60.00	$ 60.00	$ 60.00		
Car insurance	$ 130.00	$ 130.00	$ 130.00	$ 130.00		
Cell phone bill	$ 150.00	$ 150.00	$ 150.00	$ 150.00		
Internet	$ 75.00	$ 75.00	$ 75.00	$ 75.00		
Subscriptions	$ 30.00	$ 30.00	$ 30.00	$ 30.00		
Variable						
Grocery	$ 800.00	$ 450.00	$ 800.00	$ 500.00		
Gas	$ 400.00	$ 235.00	$ 400.00	$ 300.00		
Utilities	$ 350.00	$ 350.00	$ 350.00	$ 350.00		
Discretionary						
Shopping/Dining	$ 300.00	$ 250.00	$ 300.00	$ 150.00		
Self-care (massage, haircut)	$ 200.00	$ 200.00	$ 200.00	$ 200.00		
Gifts	$ 100.00	$ 150.00	$ 100.00	$ 100.00		
TOTAL EXPENSES	$ 4,995.00	$ 4,480.00	$ 4,995.00	$ 4,445.00	$ 9,990.00	$ 8,925.00
DISCRETIONARY INCOME	$ 505.00	$ 1,220.00	$ 505.00	$ 1,055.00	$ 1,010.00	$ 2,275.00

Figure 3.2. Annual tracking of month by month budget compliance with fictional figures.

To create your budget, you need to first determine your base net income for the month (i.e., "your take-home pay," or your income after all the deductions). Calculate your monthly income based on how often you get your paycheck. If you get a paycheck every two weeks, then divide your net annual salary by 26, which is the number of pay periods. If you get it twice a month, then add your net pay from those two. If you have multiple sources of income, do the same calculation for each source, and then take the sum of all.

After you identify your net income for the month, you will need your total monthly expense. This is how much you spend a month on your fixed and variable expenses. Remember, "fixed" means numbers that do not change from month to month, such as rent or mortgage payments and most utility bills (to find your monthly expense for bills that occur periodically, then divide that expense by the number of months in that period. This will give you the monthly cost for that expense).

After you determine your fixed monthly expenses, you need to estimate your monthly average for your variable expenses. Examples of variable expenses include groceries, dining, and gas for vehicles. Include some utilities, like electricity, here because if you are like me, you may pay higher usage rate in the winter than in the summer to heat your home. To determine your average monthly cost, sum up how much you spent for each variable expense each month over a period, and then divide that summation by the number of months in the period. Doing this over a 12-month period will give you a more reflective average than one calculated on a 3 or 4-month period.

Next, subtract the sum of your total monthly expenses from the sum of your total monthly income. The resulting difference may be net-negative (meaning your expenses exceed your income), net-zero (you use all your income to cover all your expenses), or net-positive (your income exceeds your expenses).

If the difference is less than 20%–25% of your income, you may need to find ways to increase your income and/or reduce your expenses. The 20%–25% refers to how much of your income you should allocate to savings, and this comes from the 50/30/20 rule that is a widely used budgeting method popularized by Senator Elizabeth Warren (Figure 3.3).

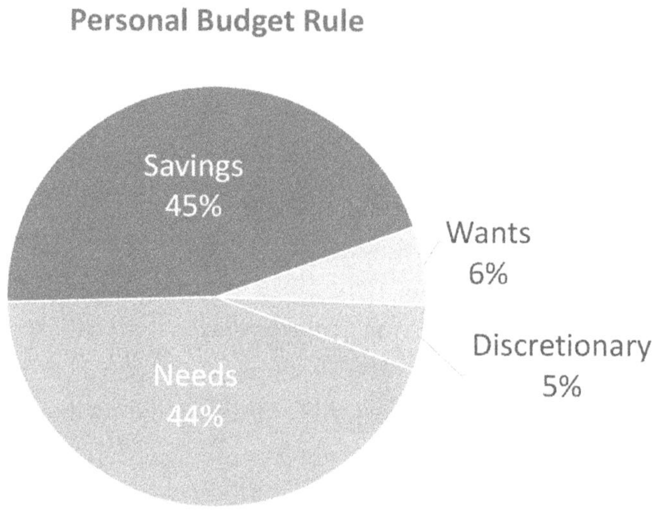

Personal Budget Rule

- Savings 45%
- Needs 44%
- Wants 6%
- Discretionary 5%

Figure 3.3. An example of a personal budget rule.

After I became a nurse and started earning money, I applied this concept to my budget, but with a different formula: 25/25/25/25 (25% each for my needs, my wants, my savings, and debt repayment). These numbers are reflective of my take-home pay, and not accounting for contributions to pension and/or other before-tax contributions to any retirement savings account. It was a well-balanced budget. I did not limit myself from YOLO-ing, and at the same time, I was living responsibly.

Budget Toward Financial Fidelity

After I paid off my student loan, I adjusted the formula to 25/35/40, where I allocated 25% of my income on needs, 35% on wants, and 40% to savings. How did I do this? I continued to live with my parents when I was single, but I helped pay for their mortgage, and I even helped with part of my dad's monthly car payment. My wants increased after I paid off my student loan. I was single and made sure that I did not sacrifice my livelihood. But even if I was spending 35% of my income on wants, I made sure that I was allocating more toward my savings account and debt repayment (this time, my BMW car).

Then, when I got married, my income doubled. Again, I adjusted the formula rule to 30/20/50. Then, when we had our son, I adjusted the formula to 40/20/40, because of the daycare needs and extra activities, such as swimming lessons, taekwondo, etc. I continuously adjust the formula that best fits our lifestyle. Just because my income doubled, it did not mean that my husband and I could just freely spend the extra money. With this budgeting framework and with coexistence of effective communication, my husband and I were able to achieve financial security. We have set ourselves up where one can stay home, if needed (and quite often during the pandemic), and still be able to afford all our needs and some wants without tapping out from any of our savings. This budgeting framework has also given us the freedom to do the things we love and add value to our life, like traveling, taking time off from working full time for more quality time, eating at fancy restaurants, etc. It has helped us achieve a life with less stress.

Once married, staying within the budget plan can be difficult to achieve, especially if one is a spender. Communication between partners is vital to stay on the course of the budget plan. Each individual needs to have an agreement and understanding of expectations and goals. Since I am the one in charge of our financial management, I make sure that my husband is aware of our budget plan. If there is a big purchase that we want to make, we talk about it and plan when to buy it. Usually we try to wait until the item goes on sale, unless it is an item that we need to replace stat or one that we know will never go on sale, like a Chanel bag, for example. The only time we do not communicate about big purchases is when we want to surprise each other, but we are both aware that we must have a fund for it ahead of time.

It is evident in my adjusted formulas from single to married life that I am always looking for opportunities to increase the cashflow to my savings account. Budgeting is a valuable tool to have in life. Without careful budgeting, it is easy to spend all our take-home income and more, which leads to debt. Saving becomes easier, and when we have a certain goal of financial saving, we start to develop strong self-discipline and we avoid unnecessary spending.

Summary

Though budgeting has become habitual to me, it is something that I continue to practice and try to improve each time. It has provided countless benefits in our life. It can be tedious or even discouraging at first, but once you continue to practice it, it will eventually turn into a habit and become effortless to

Budget Toward Financial Fidelity

do. Budgeting does not only promote healthy living, but it is also a preventative measure for debt-itis. It has helped me live a less stressful life by proactively addressing any financial risk(s) and potential issues to avoid it from becoming a chronic issue. Budgeting takes organization, time, and patience.

CHAPTER 4

Buyer Be[a]ware of Financial Waste

Healthy Financial Habit

Financial waste refers to unmonitored and unnecessary spending or purchases. Rely on your budget to help finance your wants. Even when you allow yourself a spontaneous splurge, you have already figured out in your head how to offset that purchase in your future budgets.

Life Inspiration

Life is full of lessons, and living is the greatest teacher. We unravel life's simple lessons through experiences. However, there are some lessons that are too complex for us to independently understand and comprehend, and they require us to seek guidance and wisdom from others. We encounter many sages in our lives. We establish strong and long-lasting connections with some, like our parents. And there are those whose fleeting moments in our lives impressed upon us profound influence.

Mr. Marshall was a teacher and the advisor to my high school's Academy of Travel and Tourism club. He frequently shared his experiences, stories, and life lessons with me and my classmates. One life lesson about credit cards left an everlasting impact and influenced my views on financial well-being. Though I do not recall the specific details that prompted him to share, one morning before class even began, Mr. Marshall started talking about the negative impact of only paying the minimum payment due on our credit card bill. He reviewed how credit cards worked and the role of interest rates in debt accumulation. He explained that paying only the minimum amount while continuing to use the credit card would only increase your credit card debt over time. This makes it harder to pay off the final balance. As an example, he demonstrated how a $500 purchase could become $30K in debt. He emphasized making sure we at least pay more than the minimum payment if we were unable to pay off the full balance each time. Although I did not fully comprehend the intricacies of how interest rates worked at the time, I eventually learned that credit card companies and banks assessed interest rates to make money off customers. I am thankful for Mr. Marshall's lesson because it gave me perspective and instilled in me a commitment to never having a credit card balance.

Mr. Marshall's lesson was also instrumental in how I managed one of the biggest financial blunders that my husband and I made. To give you some context, my husband is all about getting and earning travel rewards points, especially Delta SkyMiles˚. During a vacation to Hawaii, we stayed at the Hilton Hawaiian Village in Waikiki and stopped by the concierge desk to pick up our welcome packet. The worker asked my husband if he was interested in earning 30,000 Hilton Honors points by participating in a one-hour presentation. Now, my husband was all about getting free points, and knowing those Hilton Honors points could be converted to Delta SkyMiles, my husband scheduled us for a presentation on the last day of our stay.

Though we knew that the purpose of the presentation was to sell us a timeshare, we were otherwise naïve to the world of timeshare presentation and the aggressive sales tactics. If you have ever participated in one, you probably guessed that our plan to just listen for an hour and earn the points was futile. Part of this was that I grew enamored with the presentation. As we listened to the presenter, I calculated in my head how we could fit this purchase into our finances. Seeing how excited I was and explaining my financial calculations, my husband agreed with my desire.

We allowed our emotions and the heat of the moment to influence this purchase. It was not until we got the final documents that I realized the financial impact of this blunder. The 10% interest rate made me recall Mr. Marshall's lesson, and rather than financing the timeshare, I paid it off in three months. We were fortunate that we had enough in our emergency funds to pay this, and though this was not technically an emergency, I determined that the benefit of paying off the timeshare outweighed the risk of having a reduced emergency fund (at the time, we had a 12-month emergency fund). This experience taught me the importance of having both a budget and financial SMART for MI goals to help guide major financial decisions.

Comprehensibility

We are all creatures of habit and have developed our habits at an early age, such as handwashing before and after eating,

Buyer Be[a]ware of Financial Waste

brushing our teeth before bedtime, drinking coffee first thing in the morning, etc. And somehow along the way, we also develop unhealthy habits as our way to cope with stress and/or boredom, and one of those unhealthy habits is our spending habits, like a nightly trip to the bar after a stressful day at work, unintentional online and in-store shopping in pursuit of keeping up with the Joneses, smoking, etc. Unmindfully, these unhealthy spending habits can lead to health problems. For example, some people resort to smoking as their way to relieve stress. We now know that smoking can cause many diseases, such as lung cancer, heart disease, and stroke to name a few. Additionally, our unhealthy spending habits have financial consequences. Without awareness, it can lead to debt accumulation, which can cause financial stress and lead to serious health problems, such as depression, anxiety, weight gain, and other illnesses.

From the moment we wake up and look at our phone (social media and website advertisements), to watching television and listening to the radio (infomercials), and seeing what our neighbors, friends, family, and coworkers have, we live surrounded by temptations that can habituate and exacerbate our unhealthy spending. It is so easy to fall into the trap of wanting what other people have, and credit cards have made it effortless for us to overspend and acquire the things we do not even need or worse, cannot afford.

O'Brien (2019) found that consumers overspend their budget by $143 each week or $7.4 thousand a year with online shopping as the primary source. Though my group of friends jokingly suggested retail therapy to alleviate negative feelings, there is some truth that retail therapy can provide immediate gratification and improve mood (Cleveland Clinic, 2021). With the advent of online shopping, retail therapy is much more accessible with much more products to select and no longer limited to physical stores. This accessibility has unfortunately also increased the risk of retail therapy evolving into a compulsive buying disorder (American Addiction Centers, 2019).

With both habits of overspending and online shopping, it is not surprising people end up accruing debt. Clearly, spending has become a habit and being in debt has become a norm. I remember a friend telling me, "It is ok to be in debt. That's how life is here in America, everybody has debt." Schultz and Sherrier's (2021) review of credit card report data between January and February 2021 supported such sentiment. They noted that during this timeframe, the average credit card balance was $6,569 and that "53% of all active credit card accounts carried a balance in Q4 2020."

The harm of carrying a credit card balance is the central focus of Mr. Marshall's lesson. Credit cards have daily compounding interests. This means that the issuer charges you interest every day for carrying a balance. For example, the daily interest rate on a card with annual percentage rate (APR) of 20% would be about 0.055% (this is calculated by dividing 20% by 360 billing days; a billing cycle usually consists of 30 days). Compound interest increases your credit card balance each day. If your credit card balance is $5,500, then you will have a daily interest of $3.03. For the month (i.e., end of the billing cycle), your total interest charge is $90.90 for the billing cycle. Your new balance is $5,590.90. If you pay $150, your new balance is $5,440.90 (assuming you do not have any new charges), and this will accrue $2.99 daily interest or $89.70

total interest charge for the next billing cycle. If you continue paying off only $150 monthly, you will need about 58 months to pay off the original balance of $5,500. During this time, you will pay a total of $3,070.94 on interest only. This means that you actually paid $8,570.94 for a balance that originally cost $5,500.

Having a credit card increases our purchasing power and ability to support a lifestyle that would otherwise be out of our reach. This is especially true among those who have FOMO. With a credit card, we become mindless of our consumption, and as a result, we sabotage our budget and amass credit card debt, which then causes cyclical stress in our life leading to health problems as stress is a major risk factor for serious illnesses. Compared to those without debt, Turunen and Hiilam (2014) found those with indebtedness were more likely to have suicidal thoughts and depression.

Meaningfulness

The realization that we initially financed the timeshare purchase with a 10% interest rate stressed me out. I do not recall whether the interest rate was ever discussed, but I was so caught up in the moment of having a "home" all over the world that I had forgotten how this purchase would impact both our short and long-term goals. The fact that most of our monthly payments were paying off the interest first instead of the principal angered me. This was one of the primary reasons I elected to pay off the timeshare immediately. This experience showed me how easy it is for us to unknowingly succumb and accumulate unhealthy debt, and how mismanagement of debt can exacerbate our financial distress.

Though you may not have an experience like this pricewise, you may have a similar experience situationally. Consumption-driven existence may have become the norm in our society, but it does not mean we have to conform to it. Our unhealthy habits are a result of our own choices. When we choose to engage in activities repeatedly, it eventually turns into a habit that is done without having to think about it. Unhealthy habits may be difficult to break, but it is not impossible. We must gain awareness of our unhealthy habits to correct them. We have control over our life, and we can change our future. We should not let our spending habits control our life. We need to be responsible and be more mindful with the way we spend our money to avoid debt accumulation. We are where we are today because of our choices and actions. We all have a choice to choose activities that are better for our health and well-being, be it physically, mentally, socially, or financially.

Unhealthy spending habits are a catalyst to credit card debt accumulation, which can lead to financial stress and result in serious health problems. Many times, people rack up credit card debt because of mindless consumption to deal with stresses in life. People engage in unhealthy activities as a distraction or temporary cure of the problem; shopping or drinking alcohol to cope with stress is like putting a Band-Aid on an infected wound just to cover it, but the Band-Aid is not really treating the real problem. To treat the root cause, we must gain awareness of our behavior. What is causing the stress?

Manageability

I have developed discipline with the way I spend my money, specifically my credit card uses, and have become a conscious spender. I know what I can afford, and if I cannot afford something at the moment, I take the time to save up for it. To me, this practice helped evade unnecessary stress. I do not need to worry about how to pay for something I could not afford. I've always viewed using a credit card without a budget plan to pay for it in full as equivalent to spending before I even earn the money or spending the money I do not even have. I hated the thought of working hard to earn money just to pay my credit card debt because I had already spent the money before I even earned it. I want to be able to enjoy the money I have worked so hard to earn and have a choice on where to spend it versus paying off the credit card issuer once my employer deposits my paycheck.

With all that said, it does not mean I opposed the use of a credit card. I use credit cards, in fact, I use two credit cards and my husband is an authorized user for these two credit cards. We put a limit on the number of credit cards we use so I can easily keep track of our spending and make sure we do not overspend. With the two credit cards we have, we treat it as a debit card. We only charge the amount that we have budgeted for to make sure that we are able to pay off the balance in full each month. I keep track of the closing date each month for each credit card. This way, I know exactly when to stop using the credit card when we've reached the budgeted amount. Take, for example, a credit card budgeted for $1,000 and with a billing cycle's closing date on the 24th of each month. If I already spent $1,000 on that credit card by the 20th, I would not use the credit card again until the new billing cycle begins. Being aware of the closing date is my safeguard to make sure we do not go over our budget. It ensures that we will be able to pay the balance in full and avoid accruing interest because, to me, interest is a way for the credit card company to rob my bank, which I am against and do not authorize. Therefore, we never carry a credit card balance.

Having a credit card and with a significant credit limit is a powerful feeling. As Uncle Ben attributably said to Peter Parker, "With great power comes great responsibility" (Lee & Ditko, 1962), and this statement is very applicable to owning and using credit cards. I believe one must have strong self-discipline and a budget plan to avoid mindless spending because credit cards have made everything accessible and have made us forget common sense (i.e., spending more than what we earn or can afford), and sadly, this has become a norm in our society. There are all kinds of credit cards out there, but I believe a rewards credit card provides the most benefit as this is a way to earn free money or miles for traveling. One of the credit cards we use is a cash-back credit card and we earn between $300–$350 annually depending on how much we spent for the year, which is free money we get annually. Who would not want that?

However, before signing up for a rewards credit card or any type of credit card, it is crucial to understand the true cost of owning a credit card. You need to know how healthy you are financially as no credit card is worth sacrificing your financial well-being, so never try to live a lifestyle that exceeds your means. Be mindful with your spending. Furthermore, it is important to know the terms and conditions of the card. Many credit card companies offer huge signup bonuses with several first-year perks, such as waiving the annual fee for the first year. Do not let the temptation of the signup bonus blind you from the actual cost of owning a credit card. Understanding the card's terms and conditions will also give you an idea of how to maximize the card's benefits. All rewards cards, especially the ones with an annual fee, are only worth having if you use the card enough to accrue points or miles and maximize the benefits it offers. If you travel a lot, it is best to have one of the rewards cards that will get you a free checked bag and help you accrue miles for any purchases. If you are thinking of getting one of the rewards cards, consider which card will provide the most rewards that you will be able to utilize best based on your lifestyle.

My husband and I continue to be mindful with our spending habits, specifically with our credit card use. We keep our utilization low and always pay our balance in full on time to maintain our credit score on the higher end. We do not buy things just because we can afford it, and we certainly do not earn money just to spend it all. We do not change our cars whenever there is a new model; we wait until it is time to replace it. I still have my BMW and it's nine years old this year (2021), and thankfully it has not given me any issues. Sadly, after 16 years of adventure with my Honda CRV, I had to let it go because we have been spending a couple of thousand every year for the past two years for repair, and it made more sense to just replace it rather than keep it. And yes, I got a 0.9% APR on our car loan for our new car.

In addition to keeping our credit card utilization low, we also keep our DTI ratio low (monthly debt payments divided by monthly gross), which is currently at 17% as I am only working per diem; it would be lower if I was working full time.

As mentioned earlier, this is one of the ways I track the progress of our financial health: the lower the DTI, the healthier our finances are. Keeping our overall debt low has given us many benefits, such as more discretionary income, consistency with our monthly retirement contributions (both employee-sponsored and individual retirement account), preparing for our son's future by opening a college fund for him, and most importantly, freedom, less stress, better overall health, and a happier life.

Summary

It is very easy for our retail therapy to escalate into an uncontrollable behavior. Greater access to funds (credit cards) and the convenience of online shopping has only exacerbated the risks. The key to retail therapy all begins with control and awareness. Having a budget provides a tool that does both. I do not advocate for a life in which you do not allow for an occasional splurge, as such splurges can have positive effects on your mood. What I do advocate is knowing the limits as to how and when you can splurge. By budgeting for such splurges, retail therapy is just that (and if you found that you had nothing to splurge on, you can carry that amount over for future use).

CHAPTER 5

Living Efficiently Through Financial Savviness

Healthy Financial Habit

Make every dollar count. Stretch your money. Get the most bang for your buck. These are three common financial sayings that basically refer to financial savviness and resource utilization. Learning how to utilize my finances and other resources to their maximum potential has enabled me to have a more efficient lifestyle.

Life Inspiration

Growing up, I was oblivious to my parents' financial situation because I was living comfortably. My late mom was a full-time stay-at-home mom, and my dad was the sole provider. Though my dad was the only provider, my parents fulfilled all my needs and majority of my wants. We lived in a nice home and always had plenty of food to eat. I was able to keep up with the latest trends (fashion and electronics), and they even gifted me a brand-new car for my 21st birthday. They never made me feel the need to work and help financially while I was in school.

When I took over my mom's budget plan after her diagnosis with terminal cancer, I found it very frustrating at the time to see most of my dad's income eaten by mounting expenses. My dad's income was just enough to cover the monthly bills and expenses. As I wrote this book and reflected on those times, I found greater appreciation for my mom's savviness. My mom was able to find enough to save and spend because of her ability to find deals, especially when it came to groceries. Her fondness for coupons and sales gave her insight as to when to make purchases. She had an uncanny savviness with her finances as she ensured she made the most of the money she had at her disposal.

Comprehensibility

You may have heard of the phrase "living below your means." The concept behind this phrase is to spend less by simplifying your life and cutting off unnecessary expenses. I will not deny that such practice has financial benefits. I am concerned, however, that a full commitment to this practice could negatively impact your outlook on life and deprive you of the ability to enjoy the fruits of your labor. For this reason, I advocate to live efficiently, and financial efficiency is an important component of this lifestyle.

Dictionary.com defines efficiency as the ability "to accomplish something with the least waste of time and effort." Living efficiently is based on the idea of maximizing and utilizing our various resources to enjoy life. A simple way to think of this financially is to consider how far you can take a dollar to maximize your savings and/or minimize your expenditures.

Let us say that you budget $10 a month for a particular streaming service. The following year, you decide to purchase the streaming service's annual plan for $90 a year. Though the annual plan has a more expensive upfront cost, it is cheaper on a per month basis. You could allocate this extra savings to other needs. By identifying opportunities that allow you to utilize your finances more efficiently, you realize that you can still enjoy life without having many sacrifices.

This is a mindset that I have adapted into my own life. The COVID pandemic turned many homes into a multipurpose unit. As businesses shuttered and work from home became a necessity, the home became a restaurant, office, school, and a gym. For one fitness company, this became a boon for business as many outfitted their home gyms with a $2000, internet-connected stationary bike. My husband and I contemplated whether this—and other high-end fitness equipment—was a justifiable investment. I am not criticizing those who purchased such equipment, but after much contemplation we decided against such an investment primarily because of the lack of space, inability to work out together unless we purchased two bikes, and monthly membership fees. I will, however, criticize those who bought the equipment and allowed it to collect dust. Physical health is like our financial health. Both require your time and your investment as you cannot become healthy doing nothing.

With our local YMCA closed, my husband and I utilized Nike's Training Club app. Though this app required paid membership pre-pandemic, Nike waived the membership fees during the pandemic. This app had a good number of trainer-led classes, and the only equipment needed was our own bodyweight or dumbbells. We worked out and still work out 3 to 5 times a week, and with consistency and determination, my husband lost almost twenty pounds, and I have gained strength, shed a few inches off my waist, maintained my less-than-110lbs weight, and most importantly, I feel healthier and good about my body image.

As I mentioned previously, financial efficiency does not mean we deprive ourselves the joys of life. Vacations are vital to ensuring we have balance in our lives and opportunities to rejuvenate and have quality time with our loved ones. But vacations can be expensive if not planned properly. To maximize our money, my husband and I like to plan our destination trips based on off-peak seasons. For one, travel during this time tends to be cheaper, and secondly, the locations tend to be less crowded with tourists.

As you can see, financial efficiency has positive effects in your life and can help promote the idea of living efficiently. We are fortunate to be in a position in which we finance our lives based on my husband's income. I made sure that my husband's income is enough to cover all our expenses. We then used my income for savings and expenses on our wants. As my husband's income grew, I never allowed our budgetary expenses to grow exponentially. This practice allowed us to live efficiently and comfortably.

Meaningfulness

"All work and no play make Jack a dull boy" is a proverb that highlights the importance of having balance in our lives. Nursing is a very demanding occupation, physiologically and

Living Efficiently Through Financial Savviness

psychologically, and nurses are at a high risk for burnout and leaving the profession all together. There is greater emphasis for self-care to counter this. The premise of self-care is to promote activities that allow nurses the opportunity to rejuvenate physically and mentally from the stresses of their jobs. Self-care is the counterbalance to the rigors of stress.

Similarly, living efficiently is a compromise between living below your means and living extravagantly that improves your financial well-being while giving you permission to enjoy life's experiences within your resources. Living efficiently is an active process that requires you to constantly consider the best way to utilize your available resources. Our resources are not financial alone but also include our time and effort.

One trip we are currently planning for is a visit to Yellowstone National Park. Initially, we had planned to fly there as it was the fastest way but chose to make it a road trip instead. A road trip would require more time for this trip, but it may be more cost effective than flying and renting a car. Though we could afford flying and renting a car for a trip to Yellowstone National Park, a closer analysis of our resources (time, money, and effort) suggested a road trip is the most efficient way of using our resources. Though a road trip will require more time to complete and increased expenses for lodging, gas, and food, we justified this because we would obtain: 1) financial savings of not having to purchase airfare and a rental car, 2) the opportunity to include additional outdoor recreations on the way, and 3) greater flexibility in planning as we are not beholden to the flight schedule. Identifying and implementing the most efficient utilization of our resources will provide us an opportunity to maximize our experience.

Such experiences are essential to our life's satisfaction, and I also believe it is crucial to our son's well-being and development. We desire to provide him a variety of experiences to gain a better understanding, appreciation, and respect for the relationships we have with others, our community, and nature. I want him to experience all that life has to offer and not just read about it in books or watch it on a television.

Ever since our son was a toddler, he's always been fond of race cars, especially Pixar's *Cars* franchise, and dinosaurs. During a road trip to the Southwest United States, we drove on the Mother Road and took a scenic drive to Bryce Canyon and Zion National Parks to recreate scenes from the original *Cars* movie (i.e., Sally and Lightning McQueen's scenic highway drive). With his love for dinosaurs, we make sure he gets to see dinosaur fossils in real life, so we take him to museums that have dinosaur exhibits; in Chicago he got to see Maximo, a two-story tall *Patagotitan mayorum*, the largest dinosaur ever uncovered in Argentina in 2014. He also got to see a T-Rex and an exhibit about Antarctic dinosaurs in Field Museum.

Our travel adventures and real-life experiences have been instrumental to my son's growth. People who meet him for the first time are always impressed with how much he knows and are usually shocked to find out that he was only a kindergartener at the time. I feel blessed to be able to provide my son with these experiences, but I also recognize that these experiences came about because of my family's dedication to living efficiently.

Equally important to these experiences is the promotion and maintenance of our financial well-being. I suggested earlier that efficiently utilizing your resources can free up more money for your trip, but what I am not suggesting is to use all the freed-up money on the trip. An example may better illustrate this distinction. Let us say that you have $5,000 budgeted for your vacation, but thanks to efficient utilization of your resources, you found deals or planned your trip such that you are now $1,000 under budget. It is tempting to use that extra $1,000 on your vacation, but what I would suggest is that you set that extra money toward savings, investments, or debt repayment.

As my husband and I are constantly evaluating our financial habits and activities, we are also constantly analyzing whether we are using our funds and resources in the most efficient way possible. I have learned to focus on the progress and to live a well-balanced life because living efficiently prepared us for the future while simultaneously allowing us to live fully in the moment without wrecking our savings or placing us in debt. This approach has enabled us to attain financial security and freedom. We can live a less stressful life as we do not worry about unexpected expenses since we have prepared for it.

Manageability

I live by the expression *"just because you can afford it does not mean you should buy it."* It is easy to desire all the things we see around us, and if we fall into the trap of keeping up with the Joneses, we become materialistic and waste our money on things we do not need. As Dave Ramsey puts it, "We buy things we do not need with money we do not have to impress people we do not like."

Living efficiently is a mindset and commitment to our financial goals and well-being, and they are essential to serving as a safeguard from all the temptations and distractions surrounding us. They enhance our ability to resist pressure from society, family, or friends to spend money on things that we do not need nor add value to our life. In return, we can make better decisions that enhance our financial well-being.

Living efficiently has been easier since we are a two-income household. As I mentioned in budgeting, we ensure that my husband's income can cover all of our essential expenses. We then use my income to fund our financial goals, such as debt repayment, retirement investments, and emergency, college, and leisure funds. We adjust our budget as needed whenever our essential expenses changes, but we never increase our expenses just because we are generating more income. This concept holds true if you are multi-income or not, with the only difference being that for single-income earners, your expenses should be based on what your income was a couple of years before.

Our reason for living efficiently is like the reason why many organizations, including the healthcare systems I work at, adopt (or attempt to) *lean thinking and practice*. Based on the Toyota Production System (TPS), lean—as first described by Krafcik (1988) and further expanded upon by Womack and Jones (2003)—describes enterprises that can produce quality products or services through the creation and utilization of a highly proficient workforce empowered to continuously look for opportunities to eliminate waste in its various forms. My husband and I applied some of the tools used by lean enterprises into our practice of living efficiently.

A core tenet of TPS and lean is *kaizen*. The English translation of this Japanese term is "good change," but it refers to the idea of continuous improvement. As I mentioned previously, my husband and I are constantly analyzing our financial habits and activities to get the greatest return. Where are the opportunities for us to save money in our current expenses? My husband is always on the lookout for any deals that involve our streaming services and other utilities. Even though my son is not yet old enough for a cellphone, my husband got him a phone number because T-Mobile was offering customers a free phone line. My husband did this because he knew my son would need his own number in the future.

Furthermore, embracing kaizen acknowledges that constant change abounds in our life, and our ability to adapt to that change depends on our ability to study and learn from our responses to those changes. Our responses may not always be the right choice, but so long as we learn from it and make necessary adjustments, we demonstrate kaizen. PDCA (an acronym that stands for plan, do, check, and act) provides simple guidance on determining how successful our responses are to change or problems (ASQ, 2022).

Just-in-time (JIT) typically refers to delivering or obtaining "the right items at the right time in the right amounts" (Liker, 2003). Applying this concept has been beneficial in reducing our waste, especially when it comes to groceries and perishables. Many of us have a just-in-case mindset in which we buy items because we may need it and not because we do need it. There are times when this mindset is necessary (such as preparing for an incoming natural disaster), but for most of the time, such a mindset can lead to a lot of waste. There was a time in which a lot of our groceries have gone wasted because we thought we may need it (especially when we used to buy most of our produce at Costco). However, we have significantly reduced our food wastage because we started meal planning for the week. This guided us in buying only the groceries needed for that week.

For non-perishable items, we "5S'd" our home and implemented our own *kanban* system. 5S refers to five activities (sort, straighten, shine, standardize, and sustain) that help lean enterprises ensure and maintain efficiency. Kanban is Japanese for "sign," so a kanban system is about using signs to notify us to restock or repurchase needed items. Utilizing both tools allowed us to forecast our purchasing schedule of our household items and avoid stockout and stockpiling items that have an expiration date. After sorting, straightening, and shining our home (i.e., we discarded or donated unneeded items, organized our remaining items, and cleaned our home), we were able to create a designated storage room for all our bathroom items—toilet paper, cleaning supplies, toiletries, etc. I categorized each item, and each has a designated bin, like toothpaste, toothbrush head refills, and dental floss are all in one bin designated for dental hygiene items, and each item has an index card tied to the last item. For example, I usually buy toothpaste in a pack of two, so the storage bin would have two toothpastes, and I attach an index card to the second toothpaste. When we "pull" the second toothpaste, we remove the attached index card and place it in a container. This container contains all the items that we need to purchase within the next two to four weeks. This system ensures we have a product on hand before we run out of it. This process provides an example of our standardization and kanban system.

With this system, we can better plan when we need to purchase our household items. It also helps me determine whether I can wait to buy the item until it goes on sale

(Costco and many other stores usually have a sale cycle). Lastly, utilizing this system gives us a better visualization of our household items and we know exactly where things are located. As a result, we avoid wasting time looking for things because we know the location of each stored item. Because of the ease of this practice, we have been able to sustain this activity.

Summary

Our practice of living efficiently prepared us well for this unprecedented time. We were able to make a decision that was best for our family without jeopardizing our finances and well-being. Without hesitation, we put our son's needs above my career goals, and because I was struggling at my job at the time (I was questioning whether being a QI Specialist was right for me), it made sense to pause my career goals and put my son first. Dealing with hardships does not have to be as stressful. I understand that we cannot prepare for many unforeseeable events, such as death, but many of these unforeseeable events will require money, such as paying for a funeral, medical bills, etc. When we maintain good financial health, dealing with life tribulations becomes less stressful, and we can focus more on dealing with the real situation, such as grieving for loss of a loved one rather than finding ways to solve the money problems.

CHAPTER 6

Save Yourself to Enhance Your Financial Resiliency and Security

Healthy Financial Habit

Financial resiliency determines how well you can manage financial stressors. One of my top financial priorities every year, and hopefully after this chapter yours as well, is to rebuild our family's savings and investments and review our insurance coverages. This is to ensure that we have sufficient funds or coverages to confront unexpectedly or expectedly high expenses or significant life changes.

Life Inspiration

Long before my mother's death, my mom got life insurance and always reminded me to save. Her desire for life insurance was to offset her funeral expenses when she died rather than to provide my father with supplemental income. Thus, she opted for minimum coverage. My eldest brother covered her monthly

Save Yourself to Enhance Your Financial Resiliency and Security

premiums since she had no income of her own and very little savings to use on this purchase.

The lack of savings played a role in my mother constantly reminding me to save for emergencies. When I started earning money, my mom always told me (in Tagalog), "Kahit magkano ang kinikita mo, mag–ipon ka palagi." Translated, it means to always save no matter how much I earn. She suggested at least 10%–20% of my annual income, but I made it a goal to save more than 20% of my monthly net income.

My mom lived for only ten months after her diagnosis with stage four colon cancer. Because she became allergic and unable to tolerate her chemotherapy, my family and I made the difficult and painful decision to transition her to hospice care. My dad retired early to devote his time to taking care of my mom during her remaining days. With my mom incapacitated and my dad retired, I—the youngest in my family—became the matriarch and inherited the responsibility of managing all their finances and other affairs. My dad's early retirement halved his monthly income, and he did not yet have access to his pension as he waited for his employer to process his paperwork.

My mom's foresight proved invaluable when she died. As the beneficiary of her life insurance, I used the $25,000 to cover all her funeral expenses, her medical bills, and other expenses. I also utilized my savings to help my dad with his other monthly expenses until he finally received his retirement pension and Social Security benefits. My mom's death was physically, mentally, and emotionally draining, but because my mom prepared me to expect financial uncertainties, I did not experience the financial stress that may have befallen others with similar experiences.

Comprehensibility

When bacteria causes an infection, it elicits an immune response from the body. Immune responses include increasing the body's temperature (fever) and activating various white blood cells to destroy the bacteria and protect the body from further harm. In addition, the body's immune system learns how to protect it quickly and better against the same type of bacterial infection in the future.

Likewise, our financial well-being is dependent on a financial immune system to protect us from destabilization due to financial illness such as unexpected expenses or loss of income. Our financial immune system consists of a mixture of savings, insurances, and investments. The stronger our financial immune system, the better we can withstand financial illness and disease. This ability is what I refer to as my financial resiliency.

Resiliency is an important concept in nursing. Nursing is a stressful profession in multiple ways. Physically, I have had times in which I was on my feet non-stop, moving from one patient to another for several hours straight. I have had to lift legs that were larger and heavier than me, and you may have heard stories of nurses who have gone twelve hours without using the bathroom or taking breaks. We find the stress compounded further when accounting various psychological factors. Some examples include a fear of making a life-threatening mistake, fake smiles when dealing with unhappy

Save Yourself to Enhance Your Financial Resiliency and Security

patients (and sometimes unhappy coworkers), and compassion fatigue. Acknowledging these challenges, health care is reliant on resilient nurses due to their ability "to face adverse situations, remain focused, and continue to be optimistic for the future" (Kester and Wei, 2018).

We need this same resiliency financially. My mom was always worried about "rainy days." Her reason for getting life insurance was because she did not want her funeral expenses to be a burden to me or my siblings. And though I used to get annoyed at my mom for always telling me to save money, I am very grateful for her persistence and not getting tired of nudging me. Because of her, I have placed myself and my family in a more prepared position financially to weather unforeseeable life events.

Many people defer saving money and long-term investment because of instant gratification; spending becomes their priority for today's enjoyment, thereby leaving a zero balance in their savings account and accumulating debt. If we do not manage or address our debt well, it becomes more difficult for us to save for retirement (as cited in Huddleston, 2020). This is a struggle that Royal (2021) highlights in his review of a Bankrate survey results in which thirty-six percent of American workers, especially those from a low-income household or considered Generation Z, do not have any form of retirement account. While some are unable to save because of debt, there are also those who do not save for retirement because of a mindset they will not live long or reach retirement age. I once heard from an acquaintance, "what's the use of saving for retirement when you will not even be able to enjoy the money or worse, die before retirement age."

I do not know the name of the show on Netflix, but from its preview, I recall it mentioning that people feel disconnected from the future which makes it difficult for the present selves to care about the future selves. This could explain why people have trouble saving for the future. Our brains think of our future selves as strangers and do not elicit the same neurological response that brings us excitement or happiness when we think about our current selves or see someone we know (Lemonade, n.d.).

I find it concerning that many people are not saving anything if at all for the future. I understand that #YOLO (i.e., you only live once) and we should take advantage of opportunities to live and experience as if you will never get another chance. YOLO is a fact that requires a disclaimer that you may also live a long time. What if you surpass retirement age and live 10 to 20 years longer, how then will you live without retirement money? Studies have shown life expectancy has improved globally. Roser et al. (2019) reviewed life expectancy across the globe and over time, and they found that we live twice as long as our ancestors. With this knowledge, it is essential to prioritize saving not only for unexpected circumstances, but also for our future, our retirement. With longer life expectancy, we need to make sure we have enough funds to last for decades after we leave the workforce.

When we invest for our future, we are letting the money do the work for us. Recall Mr. Marshall's lesson about credit card debt. The debt exacerbates all because of compounding interest. In that scenario, compounding interest is our enemy. However, compounding interest can also be our ally. Whether correctly attributed to Albert Einstein or not, describing compounding interest as the eighth wonder of the world with the follow-up statement, "He who understands it, earns it; he who doesn't pays for it," perfectly reflects and summarizes compounding interests' complexity and duality in our lives. Compounding interest can either help you build wealth by allowing compounding interest to work for you in receiving interest on investments (money makes money through earning interest), or hurt your financial health by incurring debt interest, especially credit card interest.

In an earlier chapter, I provided an example of how compounding interest resulted with you spending $3,900 more on a $5,500 credit card balance. Let me now describe how compounding interest is beneficial to us. If you invested (e.g., in a savings account, certificate of deposit, retirement account, or stock markets) $5,500 that had a historic 7% return on investment, and allowed it to compound interest for 58 months, you would earn a total interest of $2,191.97. If on top of it, you invested an additional $150 a month for 58 months, your balance would be $17,999.01. You can either allow compounding interest to work for you or against you.

Meaningfulness

The coronavirus pandemic that we are still dealing with is a perfect example that reflects the importance of financial resiliency. The shutdown during the pandemic resulted in the layoff or furlough of many people. Many working parents, especially working moms, had to quit their job to care for their children due to childcare or school closure. This pandemic did not impact my family as severely as others partly because my husband and I are both nurses. However, I did stop working full time due to my son's school moving to full-time remote learning. We did lose some income because of this, but as I have mentioned in previous chapters, I have budgeted our finances to be dependent on one income.

My greatest concern was our physical health and the worry of contracting the virus. I was most worried for my husband, who was working in the critical care unit and directly caring for patients with COVID. However, long before the pandemic started, we ensured we had at least six months of savings to cover all expenses in case we had a loss of income. In addition, we both bought life insurance to provide the surviving spouse and our son financial support for five years. The thought that we may need to tap our emergency funds or cash in on either of our life insurance policies never crossed our minds during the pandemic, but as I write this book, it provides me financial solace knowing we were prepared.

Though we had managed to stay safe from COVID, our savings protected us from other setbacks we experienced during the pandemic. In February 2020, we bought a new car as my 2004 Honda CR-V (my parents' 21st birthday gift for me) finally gave in, and my husband had to deal with a severe eye infection for three weeks. This past year, 2021, has not been that smooth either. We: 1) replaced a window and then later bought a new tire for our new car, 2) dealt with my husband's reoccurrence of his eye infection and treated his second-degree burn he sustained from baking a dessert, 3) took my son to the emergency room to manage a severe allergic reaction to a friend's dog, and 4) grieved the deaths of my grandma, a close friend's father, and my husband's cousin.

Save Yourself to Enhance Your Financial Resiliency and Security

If it were not for our savings, I think I would have had an emotional breakdown dealing with one event after another. Our savings allowed us to pay off these expenses immediately and send financial support to our family and friends to help offset funeral costs. Because we have prioritized saving money for the unforeseeable life events, we are able to deal with the issue in a timely manner, and not wait until we come up with money. Our life becomes less stressful knowing we can get through any hardships that may occur because we have prepared for it. And when we are less stressed, our health is better, and better health saves us money in the long run because we avoid unnecessary visits to our doctor's office, which can be costly. Saving money helps us live in the moment and live happier. It provides us a peace of mind and helps us worry less about tomorrow because we have prepared for it. Although financial resiliency seems more apt to acute incidents, financial resiliency also helps prepare for long-term planning.

I mentioned earlier that financial resiliency is like our body's immune system. But I should take a moment and specify this even further. The body has two types of immunity, passive and active. Passive immunity is when our body receives antibodies from another source. With passive immunity, the protection will last as long as the antibodies remain because the body cannot naturally replenish it. On the other hand, active immunity refers to our body developing its own antibodies from exposure to an antigen. The antibodies from active immunity provide long-term protection because the body knows how to make those antibodies. That is, if a pathogen infects your body again, your body can respond quickly to the threat as it has the blueprints necessary to make the antibodies.

The COVID pandemic provides real-life examples of these different types of immunity in action to treat and prevent COVID. The use of monoclonal antibodies is an example of passive immunity because an individual gets it AFTER they have a COVID infection. These patients require these monoclonal antibodies because the infected person's active immunity has not yet developed enough of the person's own antibodies to fight off the infection. Meanwhile, a COVID vaccine provides an individual with active immunity because the individual's body learns to develop antibodies to the coronavirus BEFORE the individual becomes infected. Because the individual has those antibodies already, the individual is more successful in responding to the coronavirus and tends to have milder symptoms than those who are unvaccinated. The mechanisms behind active versus passive immunity highlight the importance of COVID vaccines.

Financially, passive immunity is like borrowing money to help pay for debt. The loan will provide temporary relief in paying off expenses, but in the end, you are still in debt. Having emergency funds is an example of a financially active immune response because you have prepared to respond to financial threats without compromising your financial health. Financial resiliency requires both a passive and active response to create a complementary system. As you will learn in this book, debt is not inherently bad; the evil lies in the mismanagement of debt. An example of debt mismanagement is developing dependency on loans to pay off expenses (again, an example of a financial passive immune response). The dependency on this financially passive immune response leads to debt accumulation, and then becomes a source of financial illness.

Save Yourself to Enhance Your Financial Resiliency and Security

Developing financial resiliency is not quick. Financial resiliency requires time and commitment. For example, saving for an emergency fund to cover three months' worth of expenses could take years depending on how much of your income you allocate to your emergency fund. An even more unfortunate reality for many individuals and families is that to have enough money to cover daily expenses, saving money becomes an afterthought.

Manageability

There will always be turbulence in our lives. Some are inevitable, like the death of a loved one. At other times, it may be something as minor as dealing with a flat tire. Much of the turbulence we experience relates to finances, either directly or indirectly, and/or as a source of origin or contribution to the resolution. Our inability to financially weather those rough patches can make even the most minor ones feel catastrophic. However, this statement begs the question, "How did I improve upon my financial resiliency?"

The first step to developing financial resiliency is to treat outstanding debt. In my chapter on budgeting, I discussed various budgeting rules that I have followed. Whether you follow Warren's 50-30-20 rule or create your own breakdown like I have, this budgeting rule also serves as the treatment plan to correcting your debt. The goal is to correct your debt as soon as possible, which means overpaying the minimum balance. Use what you have budgeted for savings for debt repayment first. The reason being is because the cost of debt, i.e., the interest on debt and associated penalties, will most likely always exceed the returns on savings. Simply, your interest rate on a savings account will never offset the interest rate you owe for having a balance on a credit card. It is for this reason that I emphasize the importance of paying off your credit card balance every month. Once you settle your debt, you can now focus on true savings.

I mentioned earlier that financial resiliency is composed of savings, investments, and insurances. Before I get into savings and investments, I must point out that insurance is vital to financial resiliency as it provides protection for the present and the future. There are different types of insurance, and there are various legalities regarding mandatory insurance for various purposes. Because insurance is an established monthly rate, I account for it as an expense rather than grouping it with savings and investments. The only insurance expenses that my husband and I have are auto, home, and life insurance. We do not include in our budget our medical, dental, and disability insurances because these are employer based, and my husband's employer automatically deducts them from his paycheck.

As I discussed in my chapter on budgeting, I budgeted my family's monthly expenses based on my husband's income. My habit of budgeting gives me a mental vision of our overall finances for the current year (my brothers make fun of me and comment how I know the exact amount of my money even when asleep). Because of this, I can forecast how much we can save for the year, and this forecast becomes a goal itself. For example, if I know we can save $60,000 in a year, I budget accordingly to reach that goal and allocate the money budgeted for savings into three different plans (A, B, and C) at the end of the year, which itself becomes the basis for the following year's financial plans.

Save Yourself to Enhance Your Financial Resiliency and Security

Plan A is a multilayer, financial safety net that covers the year's expected expenses (e.g., car's registration tabs, taxes), unexpected expenses (e.g., home and auto repairs), and an emergency fund that will provide us living expenses for six months (it was a year's worth prior to writing this book and we decided to invest the other half in stocks) in the event we suffered a loss of income. This approach gives us some flexibility in how we manage expected and unexpected costs, but we prioritize replenishing these funds first whenever we tap into them. We also carry these funds over every year.

So why do I have a multilayer financial safety net? The reason for this is because of the type of savings account I utilize. A regular savings account offers great liquidity, i.e., we can easily and immediately attain cash we own simply by withdrawing it from the bank or ATM. However, a savings account has horrible interest rates. Certificate of deposit (CD) is a bank product that offers the saver with better interest rates because it requires the deposit to remain with the bank until it reaches a term of maturity. Because of this maturity term, CD is less liquid than a regular savings account. My Plan A takes advantage of both account types. Knowing that we do not need our emergency funds right away, we place it in a CD to earn higher interest.

Plan B savings is for leisure and our vacation fund for the entire year, which we also replenish each year. It is vital for us to take vacations every year because as adults, we have a tough task in balancing our responsibilities to work, social life, and our own well-being. As our responsibilities grow, so, too, does our stress. As the stress piles on, our breaking point begins to thin. Amid our busy lives, it is essential to make time to escape reality, relieve our stresses, and rejuvenate our being. In return, this will help maintain healthy relationships with those closest to us. My husband and I have always made it a necessity to celebrate important milestones as vacation trips. In doing so, we ensure we have at least one trip a year that allows us to reset and refresh our lives.

Plan C is for the current year's financial goal, like an emergency fund, a yearlong adventure, startup amount for our son's college fund, paying off student loan, down payment for a home, charity program fund, paying off our current home, etc. We direct Plan C toward future planning and big dreams in addition to our retirement savings. By dividing our yearly total amount of saving into these three categories, we ensure our tomorrow's financial need, enjoyment of our present life, and achievement of our goals and dreams in preparation for our future.

Included within Plan C is our retirement. Both my husband and I religiously save for our retirement and have started doing so before we even started dating. After getting married, we became more aggressive with our retirement contribution, saving at least 10%–15% of our gross income to our employee-sponsored retirement plan, and recently maxed out our contribution as our income increased. We review our Plan C annually to ensure that our retirement strategy makes sense for us in the context of the present. Our strategy is a balance between our future and present financial needs and obligations. We want to be able to live comfortably today and tomorrow, and not be rich in retirement and poor in the present.

Something we started doing more since the pandemic began was investing in the stock market. Our stock investments consist primarily of exchange-traded funds (ETF) and high-dividend stocks. We continue to equip ourselves with the knowledge and skills to nurse our finances by reading books about money management and investing and staying up to date with the money market performance so that we know when to snag stocks on sale. This does not necessarily mean we time the market; it is hard to time the market. But when the market is down, we see it as an opportunity to use our extra money for investments at discounted prices.

We regularly evaluate our financial management and adjust accordingly, such as modifying our budget plan, increasing our retirement contribution, and investing more in the stock market. During the pandemic, instead of scrolling through Instagram posts, I spent my time reading books and articles about money. In return, I have become more financially literate and learned a few ways to grow the asset side of our personal financial statement.

One life-changing knowledge I gained from reading is I finally have a better grasp of the key difference between saving money in the bank and investing in the stock market. Saving money in the bank is risk free, but it does not earn as much money (during the pandemic, the APR rates for CD was down to half a percent, when it's usually 2.5%–3%), whereas investing in the stock market has a risk to volatility but it provides a higher rate of return, especially long-term investments. Saving money alone is not enough to create wealth, but investing money will help us grow our money because of compounding interest; the money we invest will earn money through interest.

I am not advising you to invest, as we all have our own risk tolerance. It is critical that you equip yourself with knowledge to help guide your investment decisions. Though, I do want to emphasize, staying in your comfort zone is not going to help create wealth. I know this because I have personally experienced it. I used to only save money in the bank because of its safe and risk-free feature, but saving money in the bank alone did not grow my money unless I actively add more money to it. On the other hand, I have investments that continue to grow money without actively adding money to it.

Summary

Through my experiences, I value having financial resiliency. This has allowed me and my husband to resolve unexpected expenses, achieve numerous short-term goals, and prepare for our future and long-term goals (e.g., our son's college tuition, retirement, creating generational wealth, and creating a charity program in the Philippines). We boosted our financial resiliency through savings, investments, and obtaining various insurance coverage. This strategy provides a defensive posture for immediate and distant future events. Knowing we have this reserve provides a sense of comfort and reduces our overall stress level as unexpected expenses can be stressful physically, mentally, socially, and financially.

CHAPTER 7

Learn to Earn, a Lifelong Investment Strategy

Healthy Financial Habit

Society places great emphasis on education as a key to financial well-being. Though having an education is valuable, learning is invaluable. It is learning, and not education, that can both indirectly and directly improve your financial well-being. Understand and realize that education is not the only means to learning.

Life Inspiration

My father emphasized the value of education during my early childhood years. He constantly reminded me to always study hard and prioritize my education because it is the only asset that others cannot take away from me. Neither my mom nor my dad had college degrees. They both grew up in the Philippines under harsh conditions, and a college education was not an option for either of them. Because of this, both of my parents worked hard to ensure my siblings and I had the opportunity to attend college. With this opportunity in hand, they—my dad especially—had very high expectations for me and my siblings to finish college.

Because of these high expectations, I sheltered myself throughout high school and even college. In high school, I did not get to go out much. I always had to go home right after school unless I had tennis practice or other school-related activities. Keeping me sheltered was my parents' way to keep me away from peer pressure and boys. A very important rule that I had to abide by was that I could not have a boyfriend until I graduated from college.

Due to my parents' desire for me to prioritize school, I focused all my energy and time on learning and studying. They did not expect me to work, even during college, which was a huge help. I continued to live with them, and everything was free while I pursued college.

After graduating from high school, I went to college with a lot of uncertainty about my future. I declined my acceptance to the University of Washington, and I attended a community college to figure out which path to take. Community college did allow me to save on tuition expenses and focus on completing my prerequisites as I contemplated my career path.

I took some computer science courses during the first two quarters of my first year in college due to my curiosity in web designs. However, I did not find joy sitting in front of the computer creating codes and got easily frustrated when my codes did not work. I was in limbo.

Then, one day, my dad, who was working at a hospital as a security officer at the time, said nursing would be a great career choice because of job security. He asserted that nurses will always be in demand and suggested that I major in nursing instead. After pondering deeply about my dad's suggestion, I decided to switch my courses to nursing prerequisites during the third quarter of my first year in college, and never looked back.

I wanted to make my parents very proud. It was my way of expressing my gratitude for their continued support and encouragement; I knew they only wanted the best for me. I prioritized my nursing school. I did not join any school clubs and basically had no life during college; I was either in a school classroom, school library, or my room, studying. And with patience and hard work, I graduated! It felt as if not only my dream came true, but also my parents'.

Comprehensibility

Although my parents have placed an emphasis on the importance of getting an education, I have come to realize that what I valued was not getting an education, but rather, it was the act of learning. Education and learning would appear to be synonyms, but there is an important distinction between the two. Education is a systemic process of gaining knowledge that may or may not be applicable to your own desire. As my parents have, society has also placed great emphasis on education. Our school system is the primary means by which we obtain our education. What people may not realize is that getting an education does not necessarily mean you are learning. In my field of nursing, I had many classmates for whom nursing became a second or third career.

More important than having an education is learning. Learning is the act of gaining knowledge through education, experience, and studying. Financially, learning is a lot cheaper than what most people realize. There are benefits in having an education, and there are studies that show that college-educated individuals tend to have greater financial wealth than non-college–educated individuals.

However, did you know that there are ways to gain skills and knowledge without getting a formal education? Certification programs are an example. Certification in a field of study provides validation that you have the necessary knowledge and skills in that field. Having these certifications can be more valuable than having a doctorate.

My dad's career is based on him learning rather than having a formal education. As college was not an opportunity he had, he could not rely on his education background to succeed. Instead, my dad took some criminology correspondence courses that helped him become a criminal investigator. My dad's willingness to learn is what allowed him to progress in life.

Meaningfulness

My motivation to continue to learn and expand my knowledge did not stop after I earned my bachelor's degree in nursing. Learning is my way of countering my lack of self-confidence, which stems from lack of knowledge and inexperience. As a nurse, I am in a profession whose competency is highly dependent on knowledge and skill. However, nursing competency is also very dynamic as new evidence or technology comes to light on how to best care for patients. Therefore, I am in a profession that requires lifelong learning to ensure that my practice is evidence based.

Learn to Earn, a Lifelong Investment Strategy

A few years after becoming a registered nurse, I sought ways to enhance my nursing knowledge and skills by becoming a board-certified registered nurse in medical-surgical nursing. Receiving my Registered Nurse-Board Certified (RN-BC) credential meant that a national organization confirmed that I possessed the knowledge and skills to be a competent nurse. Getting this certification also gave me a pay raise.

Patricia Benner (1982), a nationally renowned nursing theorist, described "five levels of proficiency [in nursing]: novice, advanced beginner, competent, proficient, and expert." Though RN-BC credentials confirmed that I am an advanced beginner or competent nurse in Benner's model, it is my years of experience in conjunction that have allowed me to operate at an expert level in nursing. To Benner (1982), this level of proficiency refers to a nurse who "has an intuitive grasp of the situation and zeros in on the accurate region of the problem without wasteful consideration of a large range of unfruitful possible problem situations." With my knowledge, skills, and experience, I taught and oriented staff members, including assistant nurse managers, on the clinic's operations and how to address problems that may occur.

Though I operate at an expert level, I am fully cognizant that I am only an expert in my specialty. For example, when I became an assistant nurse manager to a specialty clinic that provided care to patients with spinal cord injuries, I knew I lacked the experience to care for this patient population. I proactively registered for classes and training to learn more about spinal cord injuries, the special needs of these patients, and how to transfer and mobilize these patients safely. Taking these classes were not a prerequisite for me becoming the assistant nurse manager, but it was something I did out of my motivation. Learning these skills enabled me to better assist the staff, especially when we were short staffed.

I also knew that as an assistant nurse manager, I needed to develop my leadership skills. The experience itself was not enough for me to gain the necessary skills of an effective leader. It was imperative that I advance my education to learn the qualities of an effective leader and how to manage an organization. I enrolled myself in an online program to pursue MBA-HM. My first course was about Managing Organizations and Leading People, where I learned different leadership style theories and became familiar with my own leadership style, which is a servant leader.

As a nurse, I am in a profession whose primary focus is to help patients. It is easy to assume that nurses wait on each patient's every need and perform menial tasks. However, nurses recognize that patients are not just the receivers of care, but instead, they are in fact an active participant of the treatment team. The true purpose of nursing is to empower patients so that they can return to their best healthy state possible. Nurses are natural servant leaders who work tirelessly on behalf of the patient and serve as their stewards.

Similarly, whenever I was the assigned charge nurse for the day—the primary nurse responsible for managing the workflow for the day—and then later as an assistant nurse manager, I took on those roles with a servant leadership mentality. It was important for me to ensure that the staff were doing well. I assisted them whenever I could and followed up with them frequently through the day. I would also relieve them of their tasks so they could take a coffee or lunch break. Their well-being was important to me because it could directly impact the clinic workflow and the patients' perception of the care they receive.

Writing this book is an opportunity for me to partake my life lessons that helped me achieve financial stability. As a servant leader, I want to empower others to nurse their financial health to live a healthy lifestyle encompassing mental, physical, social, and financial well-being.

Manageability

As mentioned earlier, when I started my MBA-HM online program, one of the tasks of my first course was to reflect on my leadership style using the CliftonStrengths assessment. The CliftonStrengths assessment revealed that my other signature theme is a learner, who are individuals who "have a great desire to learn and want to continuously improve" (Ramos, 2019). To me, life is a continuous learning process and discovering new things. Even though I have already earned a master's degree, I continue to learn, especially about self-development and financial management. Since the pandemic, I have set a goal to read three to four books monthly. I have found reading as my place of solitude, enriching to the soul.

While obtaining my MBA-HM, I learned about the value of money. It's already my practice to budget and save consistently, but I wanted to learn more about building wealth. My business analyst calculator revealed that my husband and I are both on track for a comfortable retirement. We even later had an initial consultant with a financial advisor who, impressed by our thorough financial management, deduced that we were in the top tier of having our financial house in order.

During the pandemic, I devoted my extra time to financial education. I read books about money to gain financial intelligence. The two books that I found helpful were *Rich Dad, Poor Dad* and *The Millionaire Next Door*. I enhanced my way of tracking my income and expenses by applying the Rich Dad's personal financial statement in my personal financial management; I sought ways to increase the income and asset column (through investing) and minimize the expenses and liabilities column (staying within budget plan to avoid debt).

Moreover, I learned to not let my fear limit my ability. The 2020 pandemic was an opportunity for us to invest some of our savings as prices in the stock market were down. But for us to take advantage of this opportunity, I overcame my fear of investing by learning more about investments and taking calculated risk.

"An investment in knowledge pays the best interest" is a famous quote by Benjamin Franklin that I use as my motivational quote to never stop learning. Education provides many lifelong advantages from acquiring knowledge, employment opportunities, higher income, to personal satisfaction and health benefits. There is data that indicates the higher the education, the higher the income—"median weekly earnings in 2017 for those with the highest levels of educational attainment—doctoral and professional degrees—were more than triple those with the lowest level, less than a high school diploma" (Torpey, 2018).

In addition, our education affects our health as seen by data that suggests college graduates have a longer life expectancy than non–college graduates (Hess, 2021). As aforementioned, when we have higher education, we have a greater chance of landing a higher-paying job, which can help us afford healthier food and a healthier lifestyle than those without the socioeconomic means (Semyonov et al., 2013).

Though it is evident that those with higher education have higher income, and those with higher income are healthier, it is vital to be aware that a higher paying job will not automatically make us wealthy, and vice versa, wealth will not make us healthy if we do not know how to manage our personal finances with healthy habits. Choosing education that yields a high wage is the first step to building wealth. Many may oppose this because of the high cost of a college degree, and many end up being in debt and therefore unable to create wealth. In my opinion, it is better to be in debt that will eventually provide a high rate of return (better paying job), than being in debt due to buying things we do not need. The second step is learning to manage our income: setting a financial goal (paying off debt), creating a budget plan, living efficiently, and saving.

Summary

Indeed, learning is the best investment we can make for ourselves. My college degree did provide me an opportunity for a well-paying occupation, but it was my desire to learn and enhance my skills and knowledge that expanded my career opportunities. Additionally, my nursing education has provided me both sense of self and career satisfaction because I am able to contribute to the community and help make a difference in someone's life.

CHAPTER 8

Find Financial Reliability Through a Career, Not a Job

Healthy Financial Habit

You work to earn income to pay for expenses, but your work may not necessarily be satisfying. It may take several jobs for you to find one that gives you a sense of fulfillment and joy. Invest yourself into that job and it may lead into a career. A job may provide income to live, but a career provides purpose and economic stability so that you can enjoy life.

Life Inspiration

"What do you want to be when you grow up?" I am sure you were asked this question at some point in your life. My late uncle asked me this question almost every day when I was about 5 to 7 years old. And my answer was the same each time, "I want to be a doctor," with my pink stethoscope toy around my neck, pretending to listen to my uncle's heartbeat.

Find Financial Reliability Through a Career, Not a Job

Early in life, we already find ourselves influenced toward a particular "career." Doctors, lawyers, and engineers are attractive occupations because they are often associated with good pay and social stature. It is only natural for parents to wish this upon their kids. Even I have found myself hinting and suggesting to my son what he should be when he grows up. However, I have come to realize that this is such a detrimental question. How can we expect a little child to know what she or he wants to be when she or he has not even experienced life yet?

I became a nurse not because of fulfillment nor purpose, but because it had job stability and reliable income. These were essential to me because my primary focus out of college was to erase my debt. College debt is a huge financial burden and is often the initial source of financial distress for young adults. The purpose of higher education is to prepare us to be functioning members of society. Yet, the one thing that higher education keeps hidden and fails to prepare its graduates for is financial management. You will find many stories on social media, friends, and colleagues of individuals working many jobs or working for many years and have yet to pay off their college debt.

The worries of financial distress impact life satisfaction. This pandemic has shown individuals with a wealth of professional experience working entry-level positions to supplement income to survive financially. A job then becomes a means to obtain income for financial survival to stave off and address financial distress. I know of many people who stay in their job because of the needed money (or to fulfill vested requirements into their retirement plan) despite how unhappy they are in that position.

I have been in a fortunate position where my job became a career. Paying off my college debt gave me financial freedom. This freedom allowed me to change how I viewed my occupation. It no longer was just a source of income, but it also became part of my identity. I sought opportunities to advance my nursing skills and knowledge. I became board certified in medical-surgical nursing, took on leadership roles, and obtained a master's degree in business administration. Most importantly, I found a greater work-life balance and discovered an area of focus that will allow me to coalesce my nursing experience with a topic very important to me, financial well-being.

By realizing that nursing is my career and profession, I was also able to simultaneously place greater emphasis on my financial well-being. I am thankful that my mom taught me the importance of saving, but in learning from her, I had subconsciously developed a fear of being in debt. Gradually, this fear has subsided as I have come to appreciate the role of debt to advance my career. This began a shift in my idea of financial well-being. Financial well-being is less about avoiding debt than nursing my finances in a way that provides personal and professional fulfillment. Thus, whereas you need a job for financial survival, a career is a prerequisite for attaining and maintaining financial well-being.

Comprehensibility

Job, occupation, profession, and career seem interchangeable in everyday communication, but therein lies significant differences between them. I think of a job as receiving pay for

Find Financial Reliability Through a Career, Not a Job

an activity that takes place over a limited period. Occupation is a paid activity that you performed or accomplished regularly. Profession is an occupation that requires advanced education and training. These describe what you do to earn income, but a career describes who you are and what you have become while earning income. It is the pride you have in your job and utilizing that experience to improve yourself so that you can be of better service to others.

My husband has been going to the same hairstylist for almost twenty years, which surpasses the length of time I have known my husband. Though her occupation is a hairstylist, I would describe her career as owner of a successful salon who loves to make her clients feel confident in their appearance.

I have been fortunate in that I have been able to make a career from my occupation as a nurse. Although many associate nurses with hospitals, you will find nurses in schools, education, and the legal community. My experience as well as my husband's hairstylist's does not suggest that a career is dependent on one occupation. If you hold multiple jobs simultaneously and find fulfillment in those jobs, you could describe your career as one focused on customer service.

A job can serve as a steppingstone to a career, but not always. You may know of people who have had multiple jobs. When I was in nursing school, I had several classmates who hoped to make nursing their second or even third "career." I marked career in quotation marks because this decision to become a nurse is really an occupational experiment. The nursing field offers stability. The experiment ends when you shift your occupational viewpoint from working as a nurse to being a nurse.

Meaningfulness

Being a nurse is an important part of my identity. My career as a nurse has had its ups and downs. Though it's typical to view nurses as those working at hospitals and clinics providing direct patient care, the field of nursing is quite vast. There are various specialties and subspecialties for nurses to focus on. You can find nurses in administration, schools, government, and even at major organizations like Amazon. What makes an occupation a career is the journey you take to understand how this occupation becomes part of your identity. This journey has allowed me to identify the best way to utilize my experience and skills.

I spent nine years in my nursing career providing direct patient care in both inpatient and outpatient settings. Direct patient care was both stressful and rewarding. It was stressful because I was taking care of patients who may be carrying the weight of the world on his/her shoulders. A lot of times they were irritable. But as a nurse, I always had to operate with an "always be kind" mindset as often we do not know what people are going through in life. People may appear irritable, and it's easier to respond with negativity. The difficulty lies in trying to determine the source of another's irritability, and then being empathetic with them. Life itself is not easy, and it can be very frustrating and complicating when we are dealing with health issues. Some people have the coping skills and support to get through life, while others are all alone or feel all alone. The rewarding part of being a nurse is simply the opportunity to make a difference in people's lives with the care I provide in their time of vulnerability.

Find Financial Reliability Through a Career, Not a Job

After nine years of providing direct patient care, I took on a formal leadership role as an assistant nurse manager and then subsequently as a quality improvement specialist. Both jobs provided me a sense of accomplishment. I had the opportunity to work with other healthcare professionals to improve the quality of care, and I felt I was helping make a difference not just to one patient, but to all those our organization served.

Though I excelled in both roles, I felt something was still missing and I could not point out what was causing the dissatisfaction. During the pandemic, I spent the tail end of summer 2020 feeling lost in my career. I took advantage of the free time I had during the pandemic and stayed in constant deep thoughts of my purpose in life. I thought I had my career path all figured out, but I guess not.

After months of soul searching, I concluded that my desire in life is to provide support and help people succeed in their roles and/or in life. I experienced this as an assistant nurse manager. I also experienced this when I became an uncertified homeschool teacher to my son when the schools closed because of the pandemic. I took the time to create weekly lesson plans that aligned to my son's interests to engage him in learning the lessons. I was pleased with the outcome of helping my son learn, as he was already reading simple sentences and knew how to subtract and add double digit numbers before entering kindergarten.

It is a very fulfilling and rewarding feeling to help someone succeed. I realized the further I moved away from patient care and my colleagues, the lonelier and less satisfied I felt with my job. After much thinking, I have a better grasp of what a meaningful life looks like to me. It is essential for me to have a direct connection, whether it be with a staff or a patient, as it is the rapport that I can build with others that enables me to contribute to someone's life.

One area I felt strongly passionate about was personal finance, or specifically, the lack of personal finance. My husband's experience with debt made me realize that there is an opportunity to formally give people an education on money management. With this realization, I set out to become a "financial" nurse.

Having a career has allowed me to identify and take on this career path without it being a detriment to my family's finances. When I first became a nurse, the primary reason I was working was for financial recovery and paying off my debt. As I began to view my work as less of an occupation and more of a career, I began to realize that as a nurse, my patients were not just the other people in my care, but also myself and my financial health. Financially, I went from paying off my debt to managing my debt to nursing my financial health.

There is a subtle but very important distinction between the three. Paying off my debt was based out of fear of financial distress. Managing my debt views debt as an acceptable part of my overall financial health. Nursing my financial health is about continuously re-assessing my financial practices to improve my overall financial health. Financially, an occupation is a means to earn income and a career is a means to manage financial health. You may know of people who stay in a job they hate because it pays well or because it provides a reliable source of income to pay off financial distress.

Find Financial Reliability Through a Career, Not a Job

As I grew into my role as a nurse, I began to recognize that my career is a means toward financial reliability. It provided me with an income to address financial distress and establish financial security and resiliency (so long as I followed my budget, of course). It was an avenue that provided professional development and financial growth. A career provided me financial happiness so that I can strive to balance my physical, mental, and social needs.

When I took on a temporary job as a Covid-19 advice nurse, though I was not able to provide hands-on care, I was still able to help individuals by being a good listener and providing resources. Many times, the callers were in high stress because of possible exposure, not knowing where to get a Covid-19 test or what to do after an exposure, unable to find an appointment for a Covid-19 vaccine, and/or needing financial resources because they were unable to work during quarantine or isolation period following an exposure or diagnosis of Covid-19. As a Covid-19 advice nurse, I had the opportunity to provide comfort to the callers and help relieve their stress related to Covid-19. Being a nurse is truly a rewarding career.

Manageability

Out of all the chapters in this book, finding a career is not a financial practice or activity. Finding a meaningful career is a lifelong practice. I remember six classmates who went into nursing to jumpstart a second or third career, and I have had many colleagues who went back to school to become nurses. Finding that career takes time, and sometimes, it requires many failures. It may not be too farfetched to say that sometimes, for you to find what your calling is, you need to first find what you do not like to do.

I believe one important factor to making a job into a career is understanding your values. How do those values align with your current occupation and career? If those values do not align or if you cannot find an acceptable compromise, this disharmony will have a negative impact on you physically and mentally (even if it may be financially "rewarding").

Unfortunately, we often sacrifice or overlook our values due to the pressures and need to address our current financial situations. In such situations, it is important to *address* financial distress first. I am emphasizing address because you do not need to solve or overcome financial distress immediately, but you must have a plan on how you will overcome the final distress. This starts with performing a financial health assessment, creating a financial SMART for MI goal, and adhering to a budget. With this in hand, you can determine how your occupation fits into your financial well-being, specifically, the financial motivation for the occupation(s).

Summary

Having a career is an essential part to financial health. As previously stated, financial debt is not necessarily a bad thing. Much of our economy in the United States is reliant on debt incurrence. We take on debt to purchase homes, cars, or start a business. Debt becomes a financial illness when we lose our ability to manage and control our debt.

Find Financial Reliability Through a Career, Not a Job

When we have a career, we find ourselves in more economically stable environments that allow for better debt management. A career provides financial growth due to annual salary increases or opportunities for vertical movement that provide higher salaries. A career also has other advantages that indirectly impact financial health, such as greater work-life balance.

CHAPTER 9

Financial Generosity, a Sign of Financial Wellness and Contentment

Healthy Financial Habit

Being financially generous has great benefits to you and society, but be generous only when you are financially content. Otherwise, though you are being kind, sharing your wealth when you do not have the financial means is a form of extravagance.

Life Inspiration

Growing up, I often observed my parents finding ways to help other people. One of the most heartwarming memories I have of my late mom occurred when I was in the first grade. My mom walked me to my first day of school when she noticed a schoolmate of mine wearing ragged and holed slippers (i.e., flip-flops as they are known in the Western world) and using a plastic grocery bag as her backpack for all her school supplies. My mom felt so sorry for my schoolmate. My mom knew I had

Financial Generosity, a Sign of Financial Wellness and Contentment

a collection of extra slippers and backpacks just sitting inside a box at home. The next day, my mom gave her my barely used pair of slippers and a backpack.

As a kid, I did not have a good understanding of giving or sharing, and I would in fact get upset at my parents for giving my stuff away. This feeling gave way first to acceptance and then appreciation as I observed my parents never hesitating to give when they could. Every time I outgrew my clothes, we always delivered it to relatives living in the province or other people they knew whose children needed clothes. Whenever a relative came over to our house asking for help, I saw my parents hand them money. My parents even helped provide jobs to people when they purchased a farm. Though my mom has since passed, my dad continues to be generous.

Now living in the Philippines, his generosity is significant, financial contributions to his community because the dollar goes a long a way in the Philippines. He made sure that the local public schools had the equipment (such as new televisions and school supplies) they needed to teach effectively so that the students could learn effectively. I send my dad my son's outgrown clothes, shoes, and toys, which he then shares with the little kids in his neighborhood. Every time he comes back to the United States, he spends his money buying gifts to give to the people in his community in the Philippines. Helping his community has been beneficial to his well-being. I see great happiness and fulfillment in him whenever he can help and make people happy with his gift giving. He always says, "It feels good to help people and the joy of giving outshines the joy of receiving." He was so lost when my mom passed, but he seemed to find purpose and value in life by helping others and his community. His reinvigoration in life with my mom's memories brought me gratification and relief.

My parents were always doing something great for other people, and that is something I appreciate tremendously from them. I learned from their actions to share with others. When my mom was still alive, we had wild dreams to help people in the Philippines, especially the underserved. We either wanted to open a clinic that provides free preventative checkup, an orphanage to help reduce the number of homeless kids, or build a school to help educate kids in rural areas. Unfortunately, my mom died too soon, and we did not get to work on the plans together to make our dream come true. Though my mom is no longer here to help me turn this dream into a reality, it remains as one of my long-term goals.

Comprehensibility

In the spectrum of giving and sharing, being generous lies in between the two extremes of stinginess (refusal to give and share) and extravagance (excessive giving and sharing). The ability to be generous, however, is dependent on your sense of financial contentment. We attain financial contentment when we recognize and appreciate that we have maintained a financial health that exceeds our needs, wants, and goals. In essence, it is *wanting* to share what you can because you have the financial ability to do so or knowing that it will not be a negative impact to you.

As I mentioned, the two extremes of the giving and sharing spectrum are stinginess and extravagance. Stinginess is the refusal to give or share when you have the means to do so. Though this chapter is about financial generosity, I am not suggesting that you need to or should be generous. Being generous must be in alignment with your core and values, and the same also applies to the recipient of your generosity. For this reason, I do not plan to elaborate on financial stinginess because others may view you as stingy when you are in fact just being selective (e.g., no one should force you to donate to a political candidate that you oppose).

I do, however, want to differentiate extravagance from generosity. Extravagance is being too generous with your wealth. This is a form of financial waste and being extravagant is an unhealthy financial habit. Many financial scams prey upon the kindness of the individual because it feels good to help and make a difference. Unfortunately, this results in depleting your financial resources and being on a pathway to financial distress if you do not recognize the scam.

To avoid extravagance, it is essential to have intimate understanding of your financial health and values. This will provide you a strong foundation to guide you on decisions that tug on your financial generosity. My husband recently received a request for financial assistance. The requester did not want anyone to know they reached out to my husband. There was a time where my husband would have unhesitatingly helped (after all, he did give his car away willingly; and without the financial resources to buy a replacement car, he ended up taking public transportation to get to work), but after I helped him overcome his own financial misgivings, my husband recognized that you cannot help everyone if you do not have the means to do so. My husband succinctly explained to the requester the reason for the denial, but also compassionately urged to requester to be honest about their financial predicament with their loved ones.

Meaningfulness

As I mentioned previously, the goal of this chapter is not to force you into sharing your wealth but to share why I feel it is important with the hope that it inspires you to consider doing the same. Nursing school can only prepare students so much for real-life application of their education. New nurses rely on seasoned and veteran nurses to truly learn how to act and think like an experienced nurse. The success of these new nurses is highly dependent on the investment of the precepting nurses and the willingness to share their wealth of knowledge.

I have this same mindset when it comes to our financial health in the context as an active member of society. The journey, effort, and dedication in attaining and maitaining my financial health allows me to have greater appreciation for my fortunes. It also serves as a primary motivator to "pay it forward."

There are many ways to share our blessings with others through volunteerism, donations, and social support. When I help others, it gives me a sense of purpose and it positively affects my happiness and health. A study done in University of California-Berkley among the community-dwelling elderly found that those who volunteered had improved self-rated health and life satisfaction and 44% reduction in mortality (Oman et al., 1999).

Since childhood, my parents instilled in me the importance of helping others, and this helped me develop a strong sense of

Financial Generosity, a Sign of Financial Wellness and Contentment

commitment to serve others. Perhaps it is one of the reasons why I unconsciously became a nurse since nursing is a calling to serve people. As a nurse, I live by the guiding question of "how can I contribute to make a difference in someone's life?" My job as a nurse gives me the privilege to educate patients about prevention of disease and promote healthy lifestyle. I can make a difference in people's lives with the care I provide during their time of need.

My devotion to helping make a difference in people's lives has given me many opportunities to extend my contribution through volunteer and donation. Before the pandemic, I tried to volunteer my time at least once or twice a year during the holiday and/or on my birthday by serving meals to feed the homeless population or donating to charities. For one of my birthdays, I celebrated it with friends by cooking and serving meals to the homeless population. It was such a heartfelt experience, especially hearing them express their gratitude. I remember one person saying, "If it were not for you, I would not be eating today." This experience helped me recognize the magnitude of sharing and being a gift to others by sharing my blessings.

As a mom, it is my responsibility to instill the value of sharing to my son, Jasper. He is an only child and I had to get creative on teaching him about sharing, beyond sharing toys with other kids. At an early age, I introduced to him the word donation as a way to share with others. For his second birthday, instead of having a birthday party, we used the money to buy clothes and shoes for donation. I know he was too young to comprehend the meaning of the word, but I wanted to introduce the concept to him at an early age to gain awareness. Since age two, every quarter, I would ask him to sort out all the toys he wants to donate. And during the pandemic, for Christmas, instead of receiving gifts, he agreed for our family and friends to donate for him to Toys-for-Tots as his way of sharing his blessings. Slowly, he is learning to understand the purpose of donating. In fact, he even asked me to add "donation" as one of the ways he can spend his money on. The story behind this is that I am also teaching him about saving money. He has two containers: one labeled to "save, spend later" and the other for "spend now for toys and treats." When he was reading the labels, he asked why donation was not on the label and asked me to write it on the "spend now" container. I felt astounded and overjoyed as my efforts to nurture him to be a person with a big heart is flourishing.

When I went back to the Philippines a couple years ago, while stuck in traffic, a kid knocked on the window begging for money for his school project. My heart dropped and could barely make sense of this reality. Though it has always been my desire to help provide school supplies, I did not realize how big of a problem it was until I heard a kid beg for money for school supplies. Before this encounter, three months prior to the trip to the Philippines, I sent money to my dad to buy school supplies because one of the purposes of the trip to the Philippines was to start an annual gift giving of school supplies, and it was also a way to celebrate my 35th birthday, by sharing with others. My dad lives in the Visayas part of the Philippines, where I, along with my son and husband, had the pleasure of sharing our blessings to one of the schools with 500 students and each received school supplies. This was also the first time

Financial Generosity, a Sign of Financial Wellness and Contentment

Jasper had the chance to hand donations to kids in person as many of the ones we've done is usually just a drop off in a warehouse, church, or a donation box. To be able to see the smile of the kids as we hand them school supplies was truly an uplifting experience, and the whole experience was even more meaningful to do it as a family.

I want to continue to help the kids in the Philippines as my way of giving back to my birthplace. After I finish and publish this book, I will be researching the logistics of starting a charity education program, Wish Upon Alice, which I will dedicate to my late mother. I've witnessed the reality that many kids in the Philippines are not able to do their homework or school projects because they do not have the means to buy the necessary supplies. It is my goal to help improve this problem, and I hope Wish Upon Alice will be able to fill in some of the gaps of inequalities for those kids in need. I am beyond grateful that my dad will be able to help manage this in the Philippines, which will be a good way to keep him active in helping the community.

Manageability

When we are not in debt, we are able to save money and have more free income, which we can share with those in need. I am sure you have ridden a plane and watched the safety video that emphasizes putting on your own oxygen mask first before helping others. Similarly, we must take care of our own financial needs first before we can even help other people. Helping others becomes easy when your personal finances are in good health, especially when you recognize that you have attained a sense of financial contentment.

I mentioned earlier that donation can come in many forms, and the idea of financial generosity is not necessarily monetary donations. Your time has financial worth, i.e., you volunteering for eight hours means one less person the organization needs to pay to perform the same eight hours of work. While understanding the various ways to accomplish financial generosity, it is also essential to understand two prerequisites to this.

The first is that generosity must be value driven (in the context of morality and ethics, not monetary). What this means is that your generosity is without expectation of compensation. Donations to charities for the sole benefit of tax relief is not value driven. The second is the capacity to give. This chapter earlier provided caution that your generosity is extravagance if you are giving more than you can.

It is one of my goals to start a charity education program in the Philippines. I value education, and it is my desire to help the children learn effectively by having the proper and sufficient school supplies. Students can have the best teacher in the world, but if they lack the supplies they need, it will affect their learning abilities. Proper and adequate school supplies will promote preparedness to learn and encourage the students to be creative. I believe the children are indeed the future of the world, and I want to empower them to learn, have hope, dream big, and inspire them to be contributors of making our world a better place to live in.

However, I recognize that my financial health is not in a state that would allow me to start this charity inconsequentially.

Financial Generosity, a Sign of Financial Wellness and Contentment

I write inconsequentially because I could open a charity now, but it would tap all my financial resources. If this charity were to go under, my family would have nothing. Starting a charity is a large endeavor, and it is easy to say "no" to this. What many people fail to recognize is the impact of an aggregation of kindness and overextending yourself.

There is a sense of guilt saying no to someone asking for help. To overcome this guilt, you must always know what your resource capacity is. Do not commit yourself to volunteer for eight hours or donate $80 if you do not have the means to do so or if it will negatively impact your own resources. Instead, offer what you can and let the requester determine if it is something they can accept (so long as the request aligns with your personal values).

I cannot speak to your personal values as everyone has different priorities, but this book can help you become more attuned with your resources, especially your finances. Nursing your financial health will help you utilize your budget to know if you have the financial flexibility to be generous. Being generous is not financial waste because it provides mental benefits.

Summary

If desired, financial generosity can provide personal satisfaction. Vulnerable people and organizations that cater to such individuals may benefit from your generosity. To prevent yourself from becoming financially extravagant (i.e., over generous), it is essential to understand whether such giving aligns with your personal values and whether you have the resource capacity to give. If you met both prerequisites and find that your financial generosity is on a regular basis, you may have accomplished or feel a sense of financial contentment. This means that you have enough financial resources to maintain your financial health and now have excess to share regularly.

CONCLUSION

My Financial Health Summary

Throughout my life I studied feverishly so I could land a successful job. Though I was not born in the United States, I dreamt of the American Dream. But what is the American Dream? According to Merriam-Webster, the definition of the American Dream is "a happy way of living that is thought of by many Americans as something that can be achieved by anyone in the United States especially by working hard and becoming successful." We perceive the American Dream as the criteria to being successful in life. But what is the definition of success? The society and media have illustrated that we can only achieve success through wealth and power, and this will provide a lavish way of living and climbing the corporate ladder. People are spending more money to own items they believe will define them as successful, even if it means being in debt. People are spending more and more hours working with a hope to be on top of the ladder one day.

Just like most people, I was striving to live the American Dream. But I had a change of heart after reflecting on what I could do to live a meaningful life. I did not want to spend long hours at work and disrupt my work-life balance. I value my time with my family. I also did not like being away from my colleagues or patients because I love working with people individually, building rapport through personal interaction, and being able to inspire and make a positive impact directly.

The definition of success varies from person to person. To many, it may be having lots of money, living in a mansion, and driving a luxury car. And to others, it may be living simply with a purpose. To me, success is continuous learning and self-improvement, making a positive impact in people's lives, community, or the world, and the freedom to spend quality time with those dear to my heart.

Our overall health is not just about being free from physical and mental suffering, it is also being free from financial misery, and therefore having the freedom to live the life we aspire. Our overall health is an intertwinement of our financial, physical, mental, and social health. The health of our personal finances impacts our physical, mental, and social health. Therefore, we must improve our financial habits to achieve a healthy well-being and live a happier life. Our financial health requires discipline, commitment, and self-awareness. You need to know what works for you, and what adds value to your life. Knowing our values will prevent us from comparing our life with the Joneses'. We all live a different life with different priorities, and what matters to me may not matter to you.

Our financial health is not based on becoming a millionaire at a certain age. Financial wellness is a byproduct of practicing healthy financial habits. I have been able to accomplish many financial goals because of well-informed decisions, devotion, and discipline. I worked hard to get to where I am today. Instead of overspending, I made conscious decisions not to go

My Financial Health Summary

beyond my budget plan. Following my plan, I found a balance between my physical, mental, social, and financial health. In this journey, I experienced many obstacles and challenges that helped me grow and enabled me to enjoy and appreciate each moment in life.

As a nurse, I focused on helping patients physically and mentally to overcome their illness, disease, or injury. I valued patients' family involvement in the care plan. Yet, I deferred the patient's financial burden on healthcare to financial counselors, insurance agents, everyone but me. In my journey, I discovered the minimization of financial well-being by society. My role as a nurse evolved based on this realization. As a financial health nurse, I hope to inspire individuals to practice healthy financial habits to improve their socioeconomic situations and contribute to their overall well-being.

References

American Addiction Centers (2019, September 16). Are you one of 20 million shopping addicts in America? Projectknow.com. https://projectknow.com/blog/are-you-one-of-americas-20-million-shopping-addicts/

American Society for Quality [ASQ] (2022). What is the plan–do–check–act (PDCA) cycle? ASQ. https://asq.org/

Andrews, A. (2008). *The Seven Decisions* [Ebook edition]. W Publishing Group.

Arnold, K. (2020, June 23). Survey: Surprisingly fewer people losing sleep over money issues right now. Bankrate. https://www.bankrate.com/finance/credit-cards/losing-sleep-survey/

Becker, S. (2022, June 3). Why are so many high-income Americans living paycheck to paycheck? Fast Company. https://www.fastcompany.com/90757629/why-are-so-many-high-income-americans-living-paycheck-to-paycheck

Benner, P. (1982). From Novice to Expert. *The American Journal of Nursing, 82*(3), 402–407. https://Doi.org/10.2307/3462928

Bureau of Labor Statistics [BLS] (2009, May 29). *Occupational employment and wages, 2008*. US Department of Labor. https://www.bls.gov/news.release/archives/ocwage_05012009.pdf

Capital One (2019, October 17). Survey reveals tension in how people think about finances. Capital One. https://www.capitalone.com/about/newsroom/survey-reveals-tension-

References

between-financial-stress-and-optimistic-financial-outlook-among-u.s.-consumers/

Carroll, R. (2018). *The Bullet Journal Method.* Portfolio/Penguin.

Cleveland Clinic (2021, January 21). Why retail "therapy" makes you feel happier. Cleveland Clinic Health Essentials. https://health.clevelandclinic.org/retail-therapy-shopping-compulsion/

The Coaching Tools Company (2021). SMART goals: Complete guide for coaches. Retrieved September 28, 2021, from https://www.thecoachingtoolscompany.com/smart-goals-complete-guide-for-coaches-with-pdf/

Dunn, Peter (2022). Power Percentage®. Pete the Planner. https://petetheplanner.com/power-percentage/

Everyday Health (2018 October 22). United States of stress survey results. Everyday Health. https://www.everydayhealth.com/wellness/united-states-of-stress/survey-results/

Fernando, J. (2021, April 01). Financial literacy. https://www.investopedia.com/terms/f/financial-literacy.asp

Gardner, S. & Albee, D. (2015, February 1). Study focuses on strategies for achieving goals, resolutions. *Press Releases.* https://scholar.dominican.edu/news-releases/266

Greene, M., Gdalman, H., Golden, E., Arves, S., & Celik, N. *The FinHealth Spend Report 2021.* Financial Health Network. https://cfsi-innovation-files-2018.s3.amazonaws.com/wp-content/uploads/2021/04/19180204/FinHealth_Spend_Report_2021.pdf

Hasler, A., Lusardi, A., & Valdes, O. (April 28, 2021). Financial anxiety and stress among U.S. households: New evidence from the National Financial Capability Study and Focus Groups. https://gflec.org/wp-content/uploads/2021/04/Anxiety-and-Stress-Report-GFLEC-FINRA-FINAL.pdf?x85507

Heath, C. & Heath, D. (2010). *Switch: How to Change Things When Change Is Hard.* Currency.

Hess, A.J. (2021, March 19). College graduates live longer than those without a college degree—and the gap is growing. CNBC. https://www.cnbc.com/2021/03/19/college-graduates-live-longer-than-those-without-a-college-degree.html

Huddleston, C. (2020, November 4). Why it's hard to save for retirement today than 50 years ago. GoBankingRates. https://www.gobankingrates.com/retirement/planning/why-its-harder-save-retirement-today/#:~:text=Higher%20levels%20of%20debt%20make,priority%20than%20saving%20for%20retirement

Hunt, M.G., Marx, R., Lipson, C., & Young, J. (2018). No more FOMO: Limiting social media decreases loneliness and depression. *Journal of Social and Clinical Psychology*, 37(10), 751–768. https://guilfordjournals.com/doi/10.1521/jscp.2018.37.10.751

Indeed Editorial Team (September 21, 2021). *SMART goals: Definition and examples*. Indeed. https://www.indeed.com/career-advice/career-development/smart-goals

Kester, K. & Wei, H. (June 2018). Building nurse resilience. *Nursing Management*, 49(60), 42–45. https://doi.org/10.1097/01.NUMA.0000533768.28005.36

Krafcik, J.F. (1988). Triumph of the lean production system. *Sloan Management Review*. 30(1). 41–52. Retrieved from https://www.lean.org/downloads/MITSloan.pdf

Lean Enterprise Institute (2022). *What is lean?* Lean. https://www.lean.org.

Lee, S. & Ditko, S. (1962, August 1). *Amazing Fantasy* #15. Marvel.

Lemonade (n.d.). The Science Behind Why It's So Hard to Save. Lemonade. Retrieved July 8, 2022 from https://www.lemonade.com/blog/science-behind-savings/

Liker, J. (2003). *The Toyota way*. McGraw Hill.

Lloyd, C., Smith, J., & Weinger, K. (2005, April 1). Stress and diabetes: A review of the links. *Diabetes Spectrum*, 18(2), 121–127. https://doi.org/10.2337/diaspect.18.2.121

References

Matthews, G. (2007). The impact of commitment, accountability, and written goals on goal achievement. *Psychology | Faculty Presentations* (3). https://scholar.dominican.edu/psychology-faculty-conference-presentations/3

Mittelmark, M. B., Sagy, S., Eriksson, M., Bauer, G. F., Pelikan, J. M., Lindström, B., & Espnes, G. A. (Eds.). (2017). The handbook of salutogenesis [Internet]. https://www.ncbi.nlm.nih.gov/books/NBK435831/

NFCC (March 25, 2019). 2019 Consumer financial literacy survey. [Data set]. The Harris Poll. https://cdn2.hubspot.net/hubfs/5146491/NFCC_2019%20FLS_datasheet%20with%20key%20findings_032519.pdf?utm_referrer=https%3A%2F%2Fwww.nfcc.org%2F

NPR, Robert Wood Johnson Foundation, & Harvard T.H. Chan School of Public Health (September 2020). The impact of coronavirus on households across America. https://www.rwjf.org/content/dam/farm/reports/surveys_and_polls/2020/rwjf462578

O'Brien, S. (2019, December 26). Consumers overspend by $7,400 a year. CNBC. https://www.cnbc.com/2019/12/26/consumers-overspend-by-7400-a-year-here-are-weekly-trouble-spots.html

Oman, D., Thoresen, C.E., & McMahon, K. (1999). Volunteerism and mortality among the community-dwelling elderly. *Journal of Health Psychology*, 4(3), 301–316. https://journals.sagepub.com/doi/pdf/10.1177/135910539900400301

Purdue University (January 2020). A surprising connection: Financial wellness and your overall health. Purdue University. https://www.purdue.edu/hr/CHL/healthyboiler/news/newsletter/2020-01/finances-health.php

Ramos, A. (2019, April 4). CliftonStrengths: Aileen Ramos signature themes report. Washington, DC: Gallup.

Roser, M. Ortiz-Ospina, E., & Ritchie, H. (2019, October). Life expectancy. Our World in Data. https://ourworldindata.

org/life-expectancy#:~:text=Globally%20the%20life%20expectancy%20increased,more%20than%20twice%20as%20long

Royal, J. (2021, November 17). Survey: More Than Half of American Workers Say They're Behind on Retirement Savings. Bankrate. https://www.bankrate.com/retirement/retirement-savings-survey-november-2021/

Schulz, M. & Sherrier, J. (2021). 2021 Credit card debt statistics. LendingTree. Retrieved July 17, 2021, from https://www.lendingtree.com/credit-cards/credit-card-debt-statistics/

Semyonov, M., Lewin-Epstein, N., & Maskileyson, D. (2013). Where wealth matters more for health: The wealth-health gradient in 16 countries. *Social Science & Medicine (1982)*, *81*, 10–17. https://doi.org/10.1016/j.socscimed.2013.01.010

Torpey, E. (2018 April). Measuring the value of education. Bureau of Labor Statistics, US Department of Labor. https://www.bls.gov/careeroutlook/2018/data-on-display/education-pays.htm

Turunen, E. & Hiilamo, H. (2014). Health effects of indebtedness: a systematic review. *BMC Public Health*, 14, 489. https://doi.org/10.1186/1471-2458-14-489

Wojcik, S. & Kang, S. (2022). Stress can increase your risk for heart disease. University of Rochester Medical Center. Retrieved July 9, 2021, from https://www.urmc.rochester.edu/encyclopedia/content.aspx?ContentTypeID=1&ContentID=2171#:~:text=Studies%20suggest%20that%20the%20high,plaque%20deposits%20in%20the%20arteries

Womack, J. & Jones, D. (2003). *Lean thinking* (2nd ed.). Simon & Schuster.

CPSIA information can be obtained
at www.ICGtesting.com
Printed in the USA
JSHW052003111122
32678JS00001B/16